The Backroad HOME

Simple Country Designs of Cottages, Cabins,
Barns, Stables, Garages and Garden Sheds
with Sources for
Blueprints, Kits, Building Accessories,
Catalogs and Guide Books

Edited By Donald J. Berg, AIA

ISBN 0-9663075-2-6
Library of Congress Catalog Card Number: 99-073030
Copyright 2000 by Donald J. Berg

Published by:
Donald J. Berg, AIA
PO Box 698, Rockville Centre, NY 11571
516 766-5585

E-mail: djberg@aol.com

Contents

About the Editor

Don Berg is a licensed architect and a member of the American Institute of Architects and of the Society of Architectural Historians. His designs and articles have been published in *Traditional Building Magazine, The Old-House Journal, Home, Hudson Valley Magazine, Yankee Home* magazine, and many other publications. He appeared in the TV special, *The American Farmhouse* on the Home and Garden Network. Don has written or edited fifteen books on traditional building and landscaping.

Other Country Building Books by Donald J. Berg, AIA

AMERICAN COUNTRY BUILDING DESIGN: Rediscovered Plans for 19th Century Farmhouses, Cottages, Landscapes, Barns, Carriage Houses & Outbuildings

BARNS AND BACKBUILDINGS: Designs for Barns, Carriage Houses, Stables, Garages & Sheds with Sources for Building Plans, Books, Timber Frames, Kits, Hardware, Cupolas & Weather Vanes

COUNTRY PATTERNS: A Sampler of American Country Home & Landscape Designs from Original 19th Century Sources

THE DOOR YARD: Old Time, Common-Sense Advice on How to Plan, Plant & Maintain a Beautiful Home Landscape

HOW TO BUILD IN THE COUNTRY: Good Advice from the Past on How to Choose a Site, Plan, Design, Build, Decorate & Landscape Your Country Home

Introduction

If you're dreaming of a home in the country, you've probably paged through all of the popular home plan catalogs and magazines. If you can't find a design that's just right, there's a good reason. The commercial plan companies only focus on the latest style, and today's style just doesn't seem right for the countryside. Miniature mansions are fine, but country homes, like country life, should be much simpler.

I find it fascinating to page through a catalog of "farmhouse plans" and another of "vacation getaways" to see the exact same house designs. I've seen the same home appear as both a "Southern" and a "Western" design. To me it didn't look like either. The idea that country homes should be generic, "build-it-anywhere" designs only works well for the plan companies. Every climate and every region has an appropriate architecture. Our vernacular styles evolved over the centuries as expressions of local cultural heritage and as the best response to local weather. They are the homes that work with nature. Think of the country and you'll think of old barns, cabins and farmhouses. Vernacular buildings are as much a part of the look of countryside as the hills and trees. When they disappear, replaced by the new generic styles, part of the countryside will disappear with them.

Fortunately, there are a few talented country architects and designers who have chosen not to follow the trend. They work in regional and traditional styles, or in their own unique vision, and create timeless designs. They draw plans of beautiful Cape Cods, backwoods cabins, Louisiana cottages inspired by Cajun and Creole homes, little New England saltboxes, Shingle Style beach houses, timber frame barns and log homes.

Their homes have porches and breezeways, big fireplaces or wood stoves, and comfortable, common-sense layouts. They are smaller than the vogue, but they probably have all of the space that most of us really need. Their homes are inexpensive to build and carefree to keep. They are not the latest fashion, but then they won't go out of style in a year or two either. They look great in the countryside now, and they always will.

As you might expect, the designers are as interesting as their creations. Most are already living the country life that so many of the rest of us aspire to. That's why they know how to design country homes. Most market their plans independently, through local lumber yards, or through small catalogs, often from their own backroad homes. Some of them are pioneering the internet, today's farmer's market for country artisans. All were quick to share their ideas for this book and generous with their drawings, but some didn't seem all that excited about being more widely known. Maine designer McKie Roth joked, "Don't let too many people know about me, or I'll run out of catalogs." Others repeated the same idea, but I'm not sure that they were joking.

Roth was a boat builder who tried his hand at home design and construction and found his calling. Louisiana designer Bob Sander's designs grew out of his love of his local culture. Architect Russell Oatman preserves New England heritage in new designs. Carolina artist David Noffsinger of Tech Art applies his sensitivity to perfectly picturesque backroad cabins. Washington contractor Craig Wallin creates the types of homes and barns that he enjoys building for his *Homestead Design Planbook*. Betty and Peter Schellens created their *Country Designs* portfolio after their success with the design of their own Connecticut farmstead. Martha's Vineyard architect James Weisman does custom designs for clients and then shares the best in his plan book. Like all of the other designers in this book, each is talented enough to vie with the best of the commercial designers and produce more fashionable and more marketable plans. Instead, each has a vision of what a country building should be, and that vision doesn't change with the trends.

The purpose of this book is to take you away from the Main Street malls in your search for a new house. Think of this as a drive to where the pavement ends, down a backroad where you'll meet country folk who craft fine buildings, and where you'll see some real country homes.

About Mail-Order Country Plans

In 1856, architects Henry Cleaveland, William Backus and Samuel Backus added a few words to their book, *Village and Farm Cottages*: "For the convenience of such as may wish to build after any of the designs in this work, the Authors have prepared careful, lithographed working drawings and printed specifications for each." They offered their construction drawings for $3.00 a set and started a tradition that continues today. Now, more than 60% of all new homes are built from mail-order plans.

All of the designers featured in the *Cabin and Cottage Plans* and *Backbuildings* chapters of this book offer construction blueprints at reasonable prices. I've seen samples of all of their plans. In my opinion, the quality of the drawings and the information presented is better than average, and as good as, or better than blueprints from the commercial plan companies. Some, like BGS Plan Company, and Larry James Designs, offer the most comprehensive drawings you'll ever find. All are of a standard to be easily understood and used by experienced builders.

In building from mail-order plans, either from the country designers in this book or from the big plan companies, there are a few things that you should keep in mind. Blueprints are rarely refundable. That standard, set by the commercial plan services, has been adopted by most of the designers in this book too. Their argument is that the blueprinting process is expensive, and returned plans are usually tattered enough to be unusable by another customer. In addition, the plan companies argue that purchase of blueprints is more like employing an architect than buying a product. The plans allow you to imagine the finished home, to see how your furniture fits, to get competitive

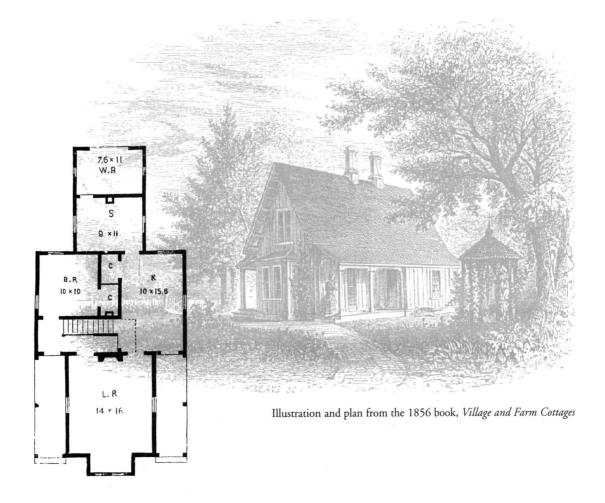

Illustration and plan from the 1856 book, *Village and Farm Cottages*

bids from contractors and to have preliminary reviews by your town's building department and by your community's planning board. Even if you don't build, they feel the plans provide a valuable service.

That means that you have to be very careful in selecting a design. Purchasing one mail-order design, and building from it, is inexpensive. Having to purchase more than a few non-refundable sets of plans is not.

In addition, most mail-order plans will have to be adapted for use on your site. At the very least, you'll need your contractor, a surveyor, an architect or an engineer to set the position of your new building on your property and plan the drives, utility lines, septic system and drainage. After that, your blueprints will usually have to be modified to suit your site's conditions and the requirements of your building department. The bearing capacity of your site's soil, the depth of winter frost, the force of typical winds and the normal amount of rain and snow in the area are all factors that have to be engineered into your building. The changes are usually made by simply adding notes to the blueprints. Your contractor or building inspector will take care of the common changes. Where more elaborate changes are necessary, you'll have to hire an architect or construction engineer. In all cases, have your blueprints reviewed by an experienced building professional who knows local conditions, before you start to build.

The Plans in This Book

The simplicity of the designs presented in this book will make modifying any of the blueprints easier and building any of the homes less expensive than with most of the houses you'll find today from the commercial plan services. I chose these designs based on their looks, their common-sense layouts, the lack of wasted space, and design elements that will make them durable, weather-tight and easy to maintain. I also tried to anticipate some of the proposed requirements of new national and international building codes and selected designs which could be easily adapted. At the same time, I tried to anticipate the future that we'll all have as we age and chose many of the homes for their open, accessible room plans.

Most of the plans and illustrations printed on the pages of this book were prepared by the individual designers. The variety in the graphics and labeling of the plans reflects their different styles.

Sizes range from 144sf for a tiny cabin to just over 2,000sf for the more substantial country cottages. The average size of all the designs is less than 1,200sf. This book starts with the smaller homes and moves to the larger ones later on. Beyond that there isn't much method to the page layout. I enjoy just reading plans and thought that you would too. Some cabins are shown with similar sized cottages. Some Southern homes are shown on the same pages as Northern ones. I hope that you'll see the advantages of each in the contrasts.

Unless noted, all of the plans in this book are printed at the same scale, 1/16" = 1'-0." Use that to your advantage. Compare rooms by size, one plan to the next. One foot of floor space on each of the plans is the smallest notch on a standard ruler. Measure your furniture as see how it fits. Measure your tractor and see how it will fit into one of the barns in the Backbuildings chapter. For some of the truly tiny cottages, there are additional larger scale plans, so that you can see the details of the layouts better.

Thanks

My sons Christopher and Ted searched the internet for country building websites. They found the "backroad" exits off the information superhighway that you'll see listed the Country Building Directory. My daughter Bethany helped with scans from 19th century planbooks. My wife, Christine, who teaches, takes care of us all, and writes on much more important matters, took the time to edit the text and better my babble.

I'm grateful to all the architects, designers and manufacturers presented on these pages, for sharing their drawings and their ideas. Bob Sander's Louisiana Country Homes inspired this book, and I thank him for that. Craig Wallin of Homestead Design offered sage advice and took the time to revise and reissue some of his classic designs. Both Andy Sheldon and McKie Roth created new designs that perfectly matched the spirit of this book.

Thank you for picking this book up. I hope it's of some help.
Don Berg, 6/27/99

Cabin & Cottage Plans

Page through the cottage and cabin designs on the next pages to find the design of your dreams. Don't lose hope if you don't see the perfect home. This book has just a small sampling of the available designs. All of the architects and designers have dozens and sometimes hundreds of other plans. Find the homes that appeal to you, and then send for the designers' catalogs or visit their websites. Read the catalogs carefully. Often you'll find that the designers will create custom homes just for you, or modify existing ones, at very reasonable prices.

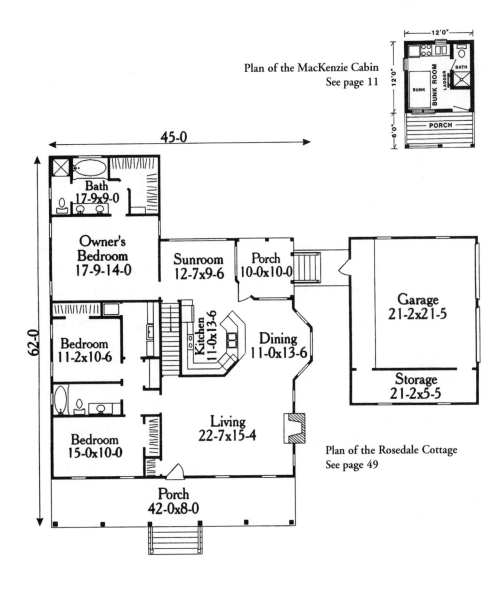

Plan of the MacKenzie Cabin
See page 11

Plan of the Rosedale Cottage
See page 49

The Saskatoon Cabin

192sf Living Space, 96sf Porch

Plan

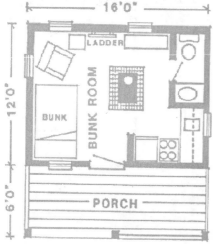

**Enlarged
Plan**

Tech Art, of Murphy, North Carolina, has refined the art of country home design to its essentials. Their tiny cabins are as pretty as any homes you'll find, big or small. They have all-purpose rooms, kitchens, baths, sleeping lofts and front porches. They're inexpensive to build and easy to maintain. What more could you want for a country getaway?

See their web site for all their designs and for information on ordering construction plans: www.grove.net/~noff/index.html.

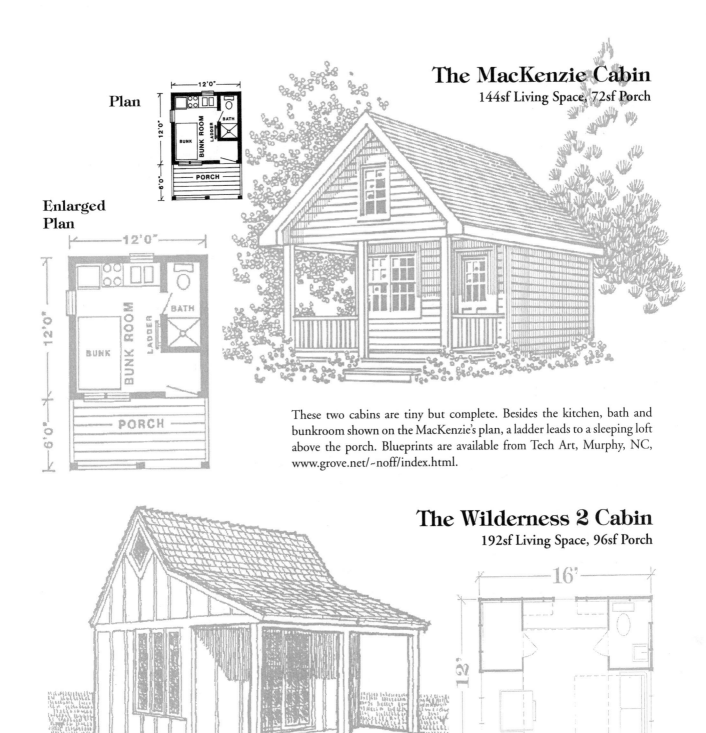

Plan

12'0"

12'0"

8'0"

BATH

BUNK

BUNK ROOM

LADDER

PORCH

Enlarged Plan

12'0"

12'0"

6'0"

BUNK ROOM

BUNK

LADDER

BATH

PORCH

The MacKenzie Cabin
144sf Living Space, 72sf Porch

These two cabins are tiny but complete. Besides the kitchen, bath and bunkroom shown on the MacKenzie's plan, a ladder leads to a sleeping loft above the porch. Blueprints are available from Tech Art, Murphy, NC, www.grove.net/~noff/index.html.

The Wilderness 2 Cabin
192sf Living Space, 96sf Porch

16'

12'

6'

Porch

Enlarged Plan

16'

12'

6'

Porch

Plan

The Wilderness 2 Cabin has areas for a kitchen, bath and a built-in dining banquette. There's room for a fold-out couch or futon on the lower level and two small bunk lofts above. Construction plans are available from Sheldon Designs, Inc., 1330 Route 206, #204, Skillman, NJ 08558. Their catalog is $7.00, or visit their website: www.sheldondesigns.com.

Cabin & Cottage Plans 11

Classic Cabins

576sf First Floor Living Space
328sf Second Floor Living Space
240sf Porch

Architect Andrew Sheldon has created a line of simple country cottages and cabins in a variety of sizes and plans. For information on his 16' wide and 24' wide Classic Cabins, visit his website: www.sheldondesigns.com.

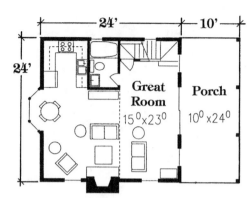

First Floor

24' Classic Cabin

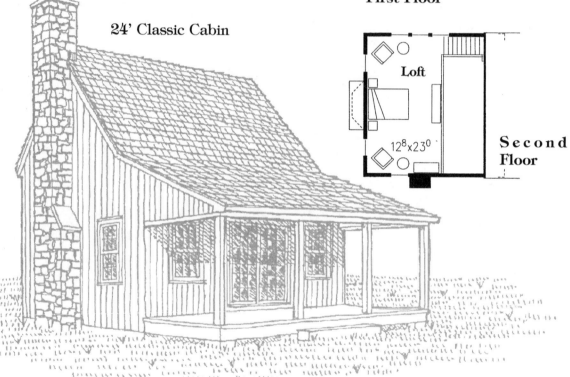

Second Floor

A catalog of cabins, cottages, barns, garages and sheds is available for $7.00, from Sheldon Designs, Inc. 1330 Route 206, #204, Skillman, NJ 08558.

16' Classic Cabin

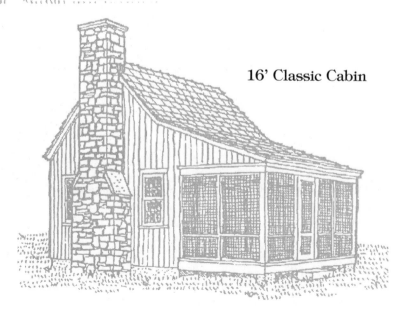

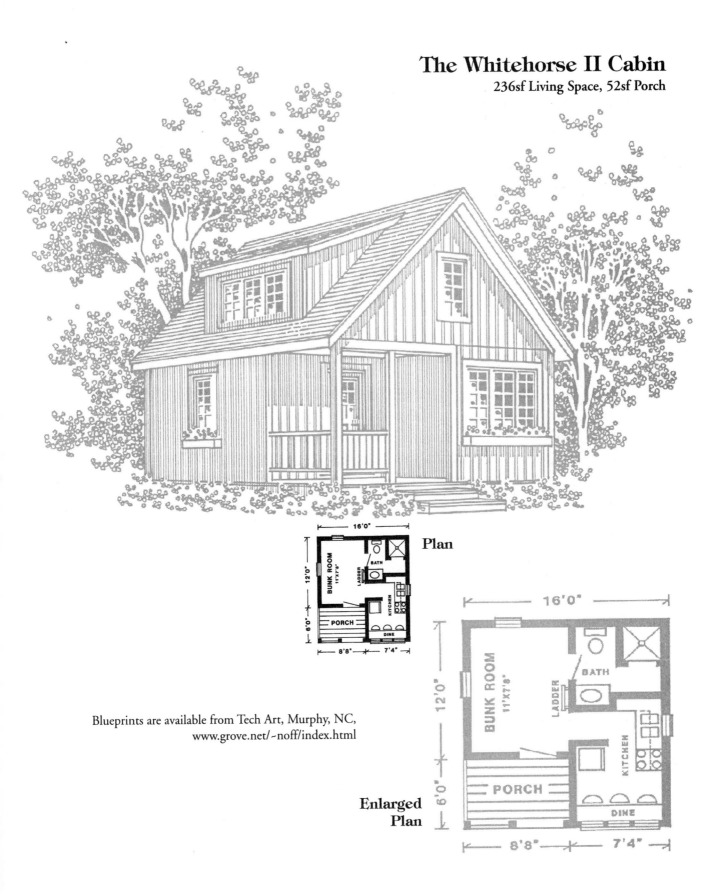

The Whitehorse II Cabin
236sf Living Space, 52sf Porch

Plan

BUNK ROOM 11'X7'8"
BATH
LADDER
KITCHEN
PORCH
DINE
16'0"
12'0"
6'0"
8'8" 7'4"

Blueprints are available from Tech Art, Murphy, NC,
www.grove.net/~noff/index.html

Enlarged Plan

BUNK ROOM 11'X7'8"
BATH
LADDER
KITCHEN
PORCH
DINE
16'0"
12'0"
6'0"
8'8" 7'4"

The Penoka Cabin
364sf Living Space, 78sf Porch

Blueprints are available from Tech Art, Murphy, NC,
www.grove.net/~noff/index.html

Plan

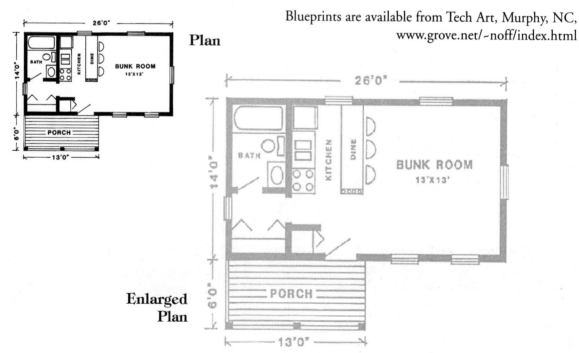

**Enlarged
Plan**

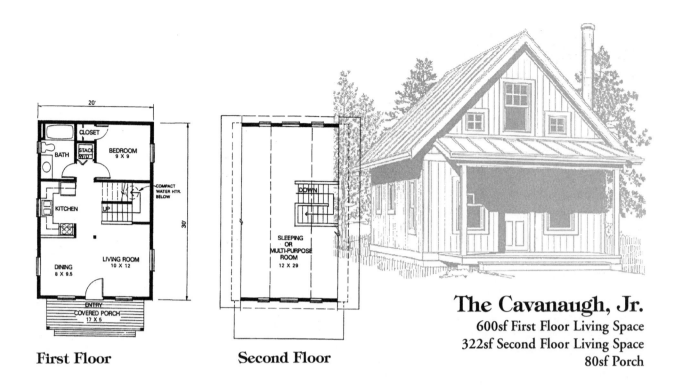

First Floor

Second Floor

The Cavanaugh, Jr.

600sf First Floor Living Space
322sf Second Floor Living Space
80sf Porch

Designer Jay Behm has a collection of efficient and inexpensive country homes, cabins and garages in his plan book. The construction drawings are guaranteed to meet your building department's approval under all normal circumstances. For more information, send $12.00 for the catalog to Behm Design, 23632 Hwy. 99, Edmonds, WA 98026. Or visit the website at: www.behmdesign.com.

The Country Bungalow II

816sf First Floor Living Space
308sf Second Floor Loft or Expansion Area
248sf Porch

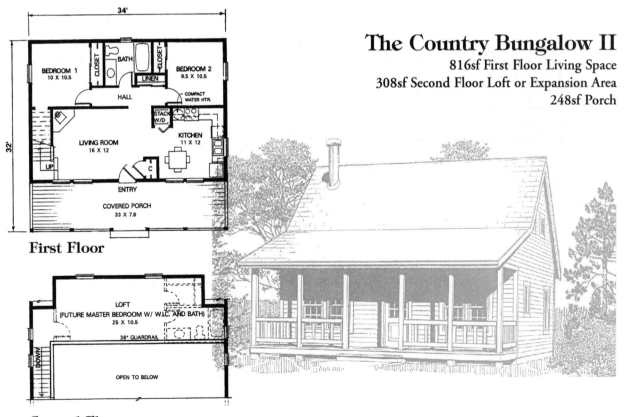

First Floor

Second Floor

Contemporary Vacation Cabin

504sf Living Space
216sf Front and Rear Porches

Log Cabin

With skylights and a hot tub, this is not Abe Lincoln's log cabin. This new vacation home from Sheldon Designs, Inc. is available as blueprints for a log structure, or for a conventional "stick-built" cabin. It can also be purchased as a pre-cut log kit. The plan below shows the 18' x 28' cabin, the largest of four layouts. The other sizes include: 16' x 24,' 16' x 28' and 18' x 24.' For more information, order the $7.00 catalog from Sheldon Designs, Inc., 1330 Route 206, #204, Skillman, NJ 08558. Or visit the website: www.sheldondesigns.com.

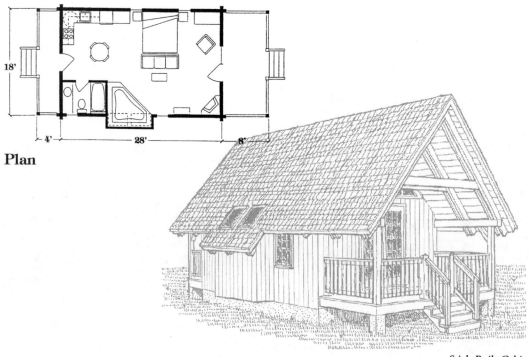

Plan

Stick-Built Cabin

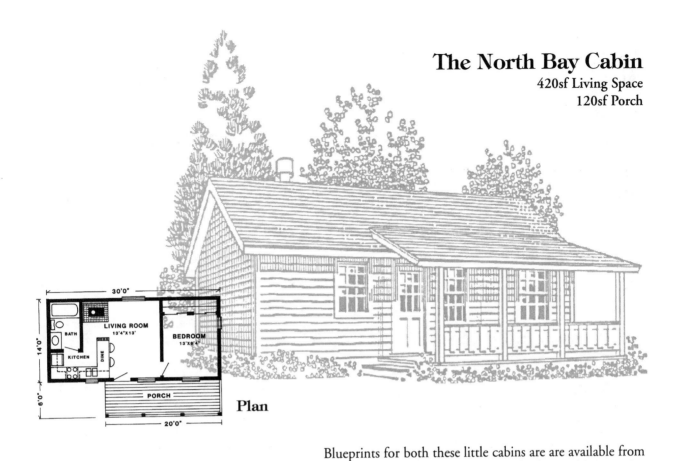

The North Bay Cabin
420sf Living Space
120sf Porch

Plan

Blueprints for both these little cabins are are available from Tech Art, Murphy, NC. See their website: www.grove.net/~noff/index.html.

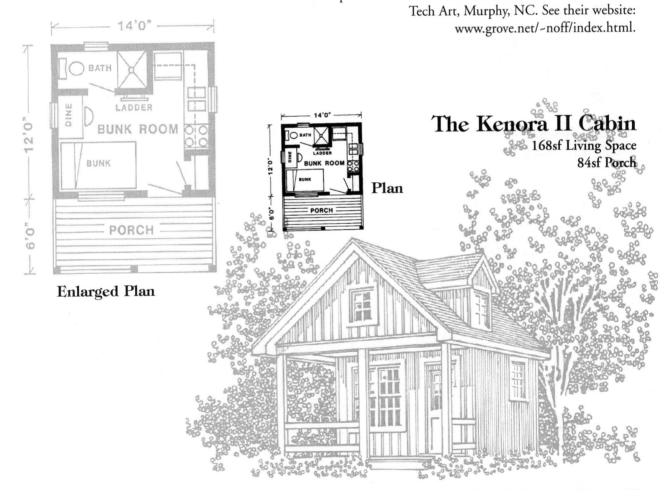

Enlarged Plan

The Kenora II Cabin
168sf Living Space
84sf Porch

Plan

The Waldheim Cottage
794sf Living Space, 170sf Porch

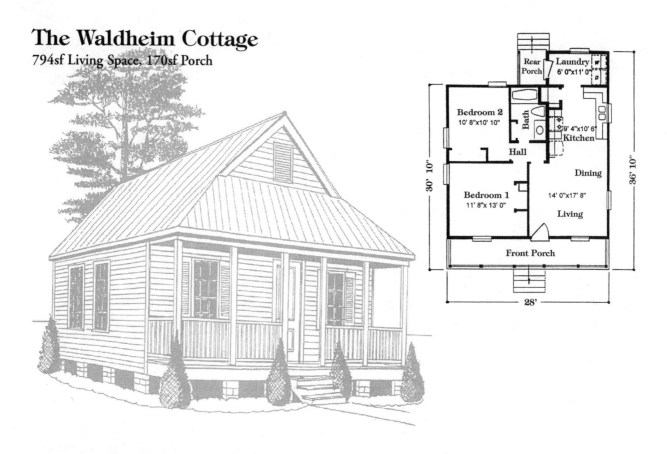

Designer Bob Sander, A.I.B.D., captures both the spirit and common-sense practicality of Louisiana vernacular homes in each of his designs. For a free brochure showing a variety of his homes and information on ordering blueprints, write to Louisiana Country Homes, c/o Poole Lumber, PO Drawer 1240, Covington, LA 70734, or call 800 525-0006.

The Oakwood Cabin
624 sf Living Space, 192sf Porch

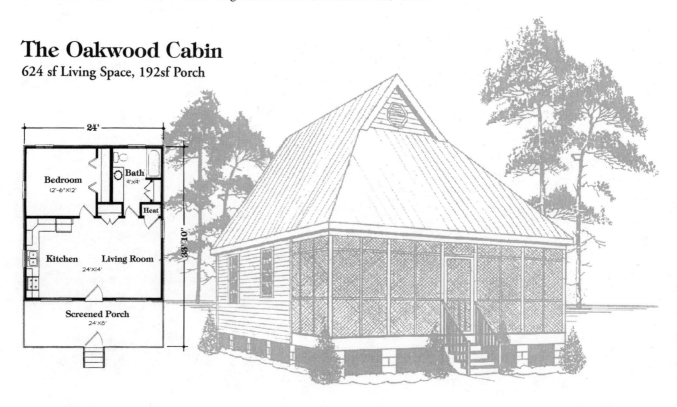

The Beechwood Cottage

600sf Living Area
228sf Front and Back Porches

Design by Bob Sander, A.I.B.D., Louisiana Country Homes

Bedroom
12' -0" x 12' -0"

Kitchen
8' -0" x 12' -4"

Living Room
12' -0" x 18' -0"

Bath
8' -0" x 12' -0"

Front Porch

20'

5' 10"

30'

Louisiana country homes are probably the most "American" of traditional American homes because they show off our melting-pot culture so well. Louisiana Cajuns are descendents of French-speaking people who once farmed and fished on the Acadian coast of Canada. The Creole culture there is a mix of different African and Native American sources, with French, Spanish and English influences. Architectural historians can trace various details of bayou homes to originals throughout Europe, Africa and other parts of North America.

The homes also show practical elements that evolved in response to the warm, moist climate: big porches, wide, shady roof overhangs and tall windows that let cool air in at the bottom and warm air out at top.

The Saphire Cabin or Cottage

400sf First Floor Living Space
182sf Second Floor Living Space
320sf Front and Rear Porches

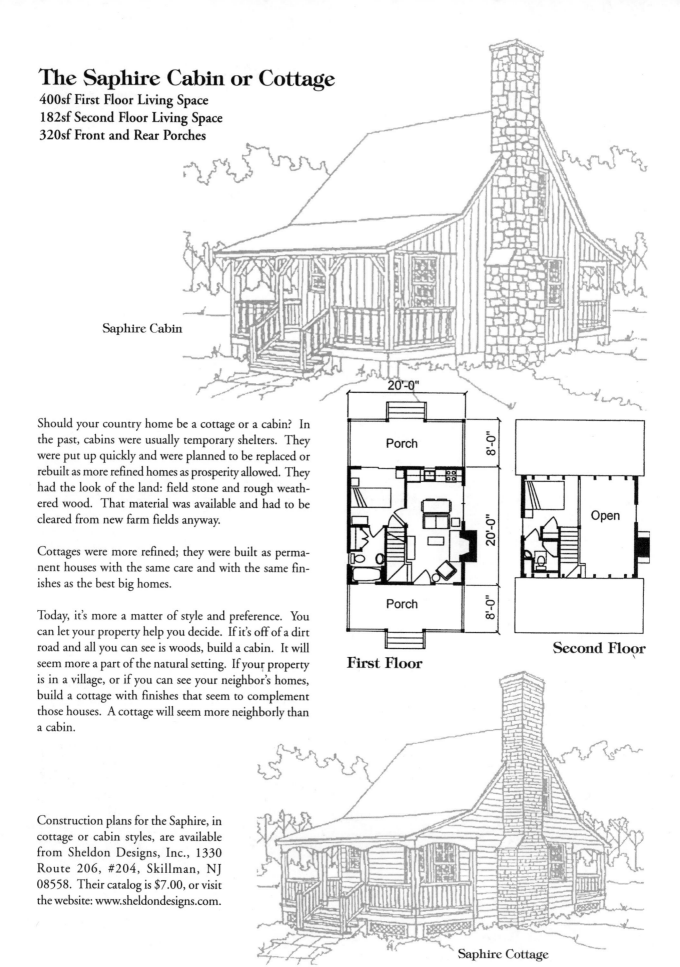

Saphire Cabin

Should your country home be a cottage or a cabin? In the past, cabins were usually temporary shelters. They were put up quickly and were planned to be replaced or rebuilt as more refined homes as prosperity allowed. They had the look of the land: field stone and rough weathered wood. That material was available and had to be cleared from new farm fields anyway.

Cottages were more refined; they were built as permanent houses with the same care and with the same finishes as the best big homes.

Today, it's more a matter of style and preference. You can let your property help you decide. If it's off of a dirt road and all you can see is woods, build a cabin. It will seem more a part of the natural setting. If your property is in a village, or if you can see your neighbor's homes, build a cottage with finishes that seem to complement those houses. A cottage will seem more neighborly than a cabin.

Construction plans for the Saphire, in cottage or cabin styles, are available from Sheldon Designs, Inc., 1330 Route 206, #204, Skillman, NJ 08558. Their catalog is $7.00, or visit the website: www.sheldondesigns.com.

20'-0"

Porch

8'-0"

20'-0"

Porch

8'-0"

First Floor

Open

Second Floor

Saphire Cottage

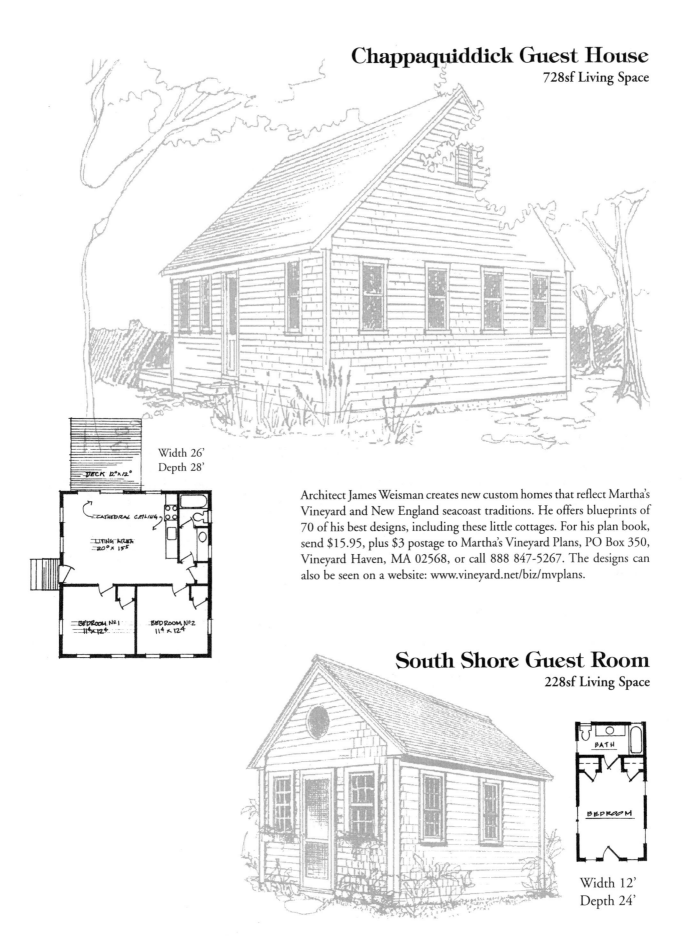

Chappaquiddick Guest House
728sf Living Space

Width 26'
Depth 28'

DECK 12°×12°

CATHEDRAL CEILING

LIVING AREA
20°×15°

BEDROOM Nº1
11⁴×12⁴

BEDROOM Nº2
11⁴×12⁴

Architect James Weisman creates new custom homes that reflect Martha's Vineyard and New England seacoast traditions. He offers blueprints of 70 of his best designs, including these little cottages. For his plan book, send $15.95, plus $3 postage to Martha's Vineyard Plans, PO Box 350, Vineyard Haven, MA 02568, or call 888 847-5267. The designs can also be seen on a website: www.vineyard.net/biz/mvplans.

South Shore Guest Room
228sf Living Space

BATH

BEDROOM

Width 12'
Depth 24'

Traditional Small House

1,003sf First Floor Living Space
845sf Second Floor Living Space
143sf Porch

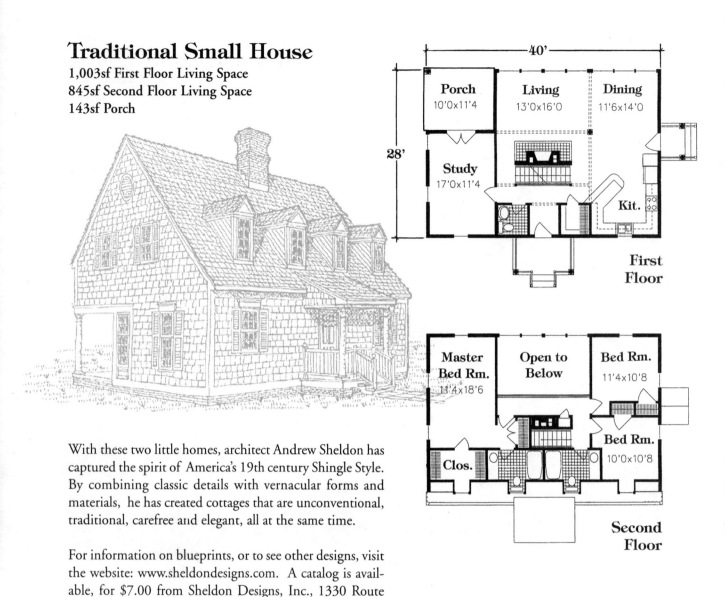

With these two little homes, architect Andrew Sheldon has captured the spirit of America's 19th century Shingle Style. By combining classic details with vernacular forms and materials, he has created cottages that are unconventional, traditional, carefree and elegant, all at the same time.

For information on blueprints, or to see other designs, visit the website: www.sheldondesigns.com. A catalog is available, for $7.00 from Sheldon Designs, Inc., 1330 Route 206, #204, Skillman, NJ 08558.

Traditional Cottage

354sf First Floor Living Space, 170sf Second Floor Living Space
63sf Porch

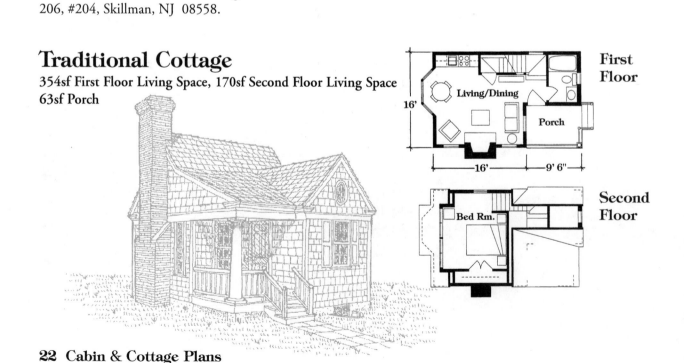

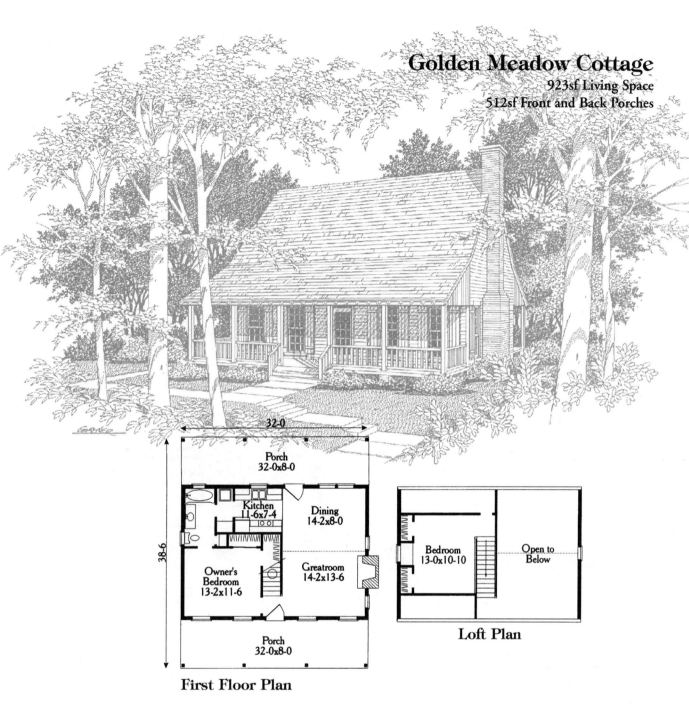

Golden Meadow Cottage
923sf Living Space
512sf Front and Back Porches

32-0

Porch
32-0x8-0

Kitchen
11-6x7-4

Dining
14-2x8-0

Owner's
Bedroom
13-2x11-6

Greatroom
14-2x13-6

38-6

Porch
32-0x8-0

First Floor Plan

Bedroom
13-0x10-10

Open to
Below

Loft Plan

This house looks like one of the pretty folk cabins that have dotted southern hill country for centuries. But, it has a modern, efficient plan and everything that today's country couple, individual or small family would need. It's one of 62 timeless country designs in the *New Beginnings* catalog, which is available for $10.00 from Larry James Designs, 2208 Justice Street, Monroe, LA 71201, or by calling 800-742-6672. Additional homes are presented on a web site: www.larryjames.com.

The Nantucket
864sf First Floor Living Space
432sf Second Floor Living Space

The Cape Cod house is a New England regional design, but it's easy to build, and it adapts well to many other locations. A West Coast Cape Cod is both an oxymoron and a perfectly sensible country home. Unlike a traditional Cape, the Nantucket has wide roof overhangs, big front dormers, and a bit of country gingerbread trim. That's Western whimsey you just won't find on a proper Yankee cottage. Notice that the windows are placed where they work best and not in the symmetrical pattern that you'd expect back East.

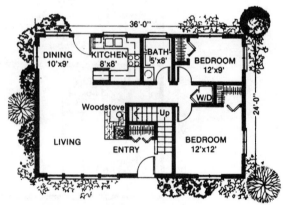

First Floor Plan

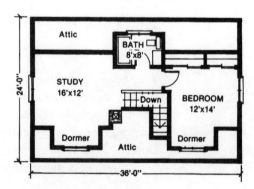

Second Floor Plan
Nantucket and Nantucket II

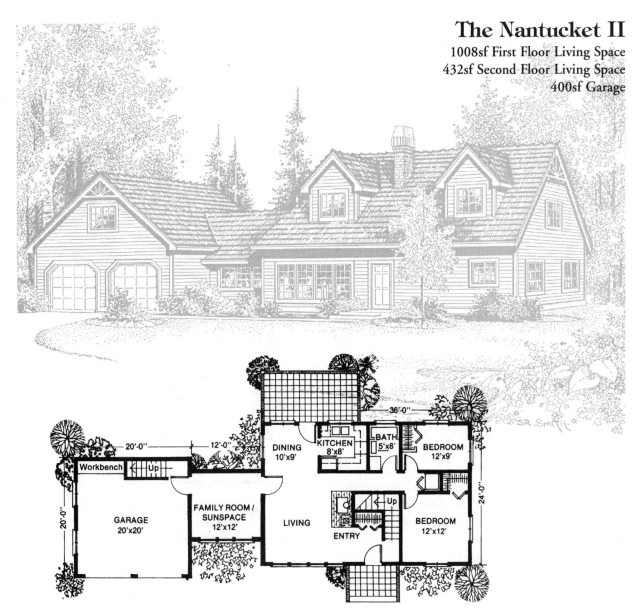

The Nantucket II

1008sf First Floor Living Space
432sf Second Floor Living Space
400sf Garage

First Floor Plan

When you plan your country home, plan on how to expand it. Over time, your needs will change, and your home should be able to change with them.

Homestead Design planned their Nantucket cottage to grow. Here it has a family room and a garage. The upper level on the garage would make a nice studio or home office. For information on blueprints, send $5.00 for the *Homestead Design Planbook*, to Homestead Design, PO Box 2010, Port Townsend, WA 98368. Or see their website: www.homesteaddesign.com.

The Brookfield House

550sf First Floor Living Space
400sf Second Floor Living Space

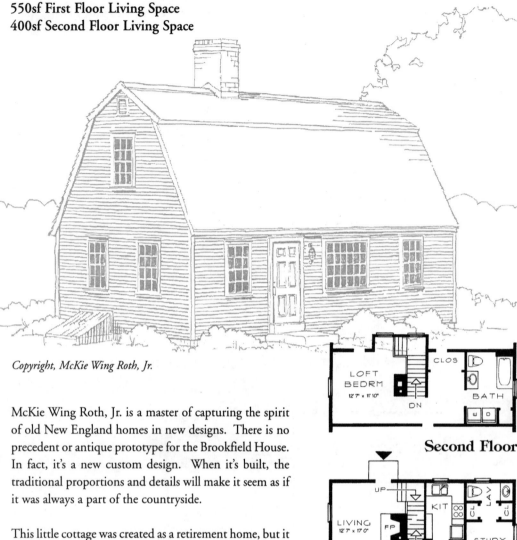

Copyright, McKie Wing Roth, Jr.

Second Floor

First Floor

McKie Wing Roth, Jr. is a master of capturing the spirit of old New England homes in new designs. There is no precedent or antique prototype for the Brookfield House. In fact, it's a new custom design. When it's built, the traditional proportions and details will make it seem as if it was always a part of the countryside.

This little cottage was created as a retirement home, but it would work well for an individual or couple in any season of life. A full basement with an outdoor entrance hatch and generous second floor storage below the gambrel roof add convenience to a simple, open plan.

For information on construction plans for this home and for 28 additional Cape Cods, saltboxes, farmhouses and Georgian style homes, from 1,380sf to 4,100sf, order Roth's catalog of study plans. *New England Style Home Designs* is available for $18.00 from McKie Roth Design, Inc., PO Box 31, Castine, ME 04421, or by calling 800 232-7684.

The Content Swyft House
1,185sf Living Space

This modern house is enclosed in a classic exterior. Two complete bedroom suites open on a generous one-room living space, with a big fireplace and an efficient galley kitchen. Everything is on one floor. This cottage was designed as a retirement home for an individual or a couple who plan on frequent guests, but it would make a fine house for anyone looking for an easy-to-maintain country getaway.

The Content Swift House is from the plan portfolio called *New England Style Home Designs*. That catalog is available for $18.00 from McKie Roth Design, Inc., PO Box 31, Castine, ME 04421. Or visit the website: www.mckieroth.com.

Two Bedroom Classic Cabin

768sf First Floor Living Space
212sf Second Floor Living Space
320sf Porch

Construction plans for this home and a variety of similar cabins are available from Sheldon Designs, Inc., 1330 Route 206, #204, Skillman, NJ 08558. Their catalog is $7.00. Or visit their website: www.sheldondesigns.com.

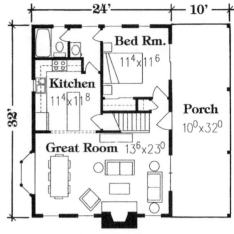

First Floor

24' | 10'

Bed Rm. 11⁴x11⁶

Kitchen 11⁴x11⁸

Porch 10⁰x32⁰

Great Room 13⁶x23⁰

32'

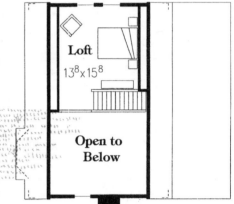

Loft 13⁸x15⁸

Open to Below

Second Floor

Cape Cod Studio & Cottage

765sf Living Space

This elegant revision of a classic Cape Cod "half house" was designed as a studio, guest house or small home. It's one of dozens of country cottages and outbuildings in Country Designs' collection of building plans. Order their catalog by mailing $8.00 to Country Designs, PO Box 774, Essex, CT 06426.

Bed Room

Terrace

B

K

Studio 18' 9" x 17' 4"

Nantucket Half House

616sf Living Space

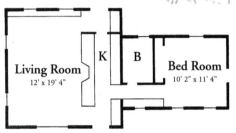

Country Designs planned this little cottage as a weekend getaway or retirement home. Both call for easy living, and this home seems perfect for that. It would also make a fine "starter" home for a couple planning a small family. Traditional half houses were designed to grow. With the chimney, kitchen, entry and bathroom all in a compact, central location, this house would be easy to expand when more space is needed. For information on blueprints, order the $8.00 plan catalog from Country Designs, PO Box 774, Essex, CT 06426.

The Hammond Cottage

1,041sf Living Space
180sf Porch

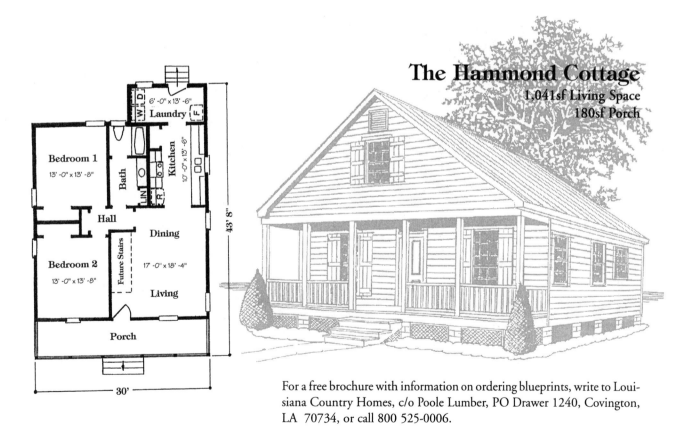

For a free brochure with information on ordering blueprints, write to Louisiana Country Homes, c/o Poole Lumber, PO Drawer 1240, Covington, LA 70734, or call 800 525-0006.

Falmouth Cape

884sf First Floor Living Space
756sf Second Floor Living Space

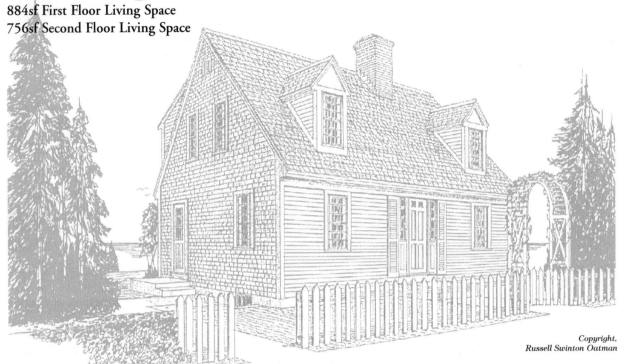

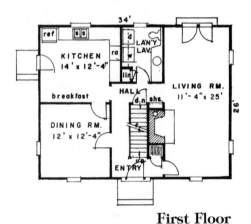

First Floor

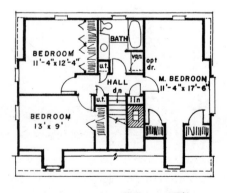

Second Floor

Called "Cape Cods" now, cottages like this have been built up and down the Atlantic seacoast since colonial days. From there they spread across the country. The roof framing starts at the intersection of the lower level walls and the second floor, making a strong, easy-to-build home. They remain popular because of the simplicity of construction, the inherent good-looking proportions and because they are easy to expand and renovate.

This is a "Full Cape" which has the entrance door and the chimney near the center and symmetrically spaced windows on either side. Smaller homes were planned so that they could expand to this final form. A "Half Cape," or "Half House," like the one on the previous page, included the chimney and door and rooms on one side only. If the family grew or prospered, the second half was added.

The the 18th century original of this house was built in Falmouth, Massachussetts. You'll find information on blueprints for this cottage and other reproductions of historic New England cottages, in *The Cape Cod Collection of House Designs.* The catalog is available for $8.00 from Russell Swinton Oatman Design Associates, Inc., 132 Mirick Road, Princeton, MA 01541.

For a free brochure with information on ordering blueprints of the Plainview and other traditional Louisiana cabins and cottages designed by Bob Sander, A.I.B.D., write to Louisiana Country Homes, c/o Poole Lumber, PO Drawer 1240, Covington, LA 70734, or call 800 525-0006.

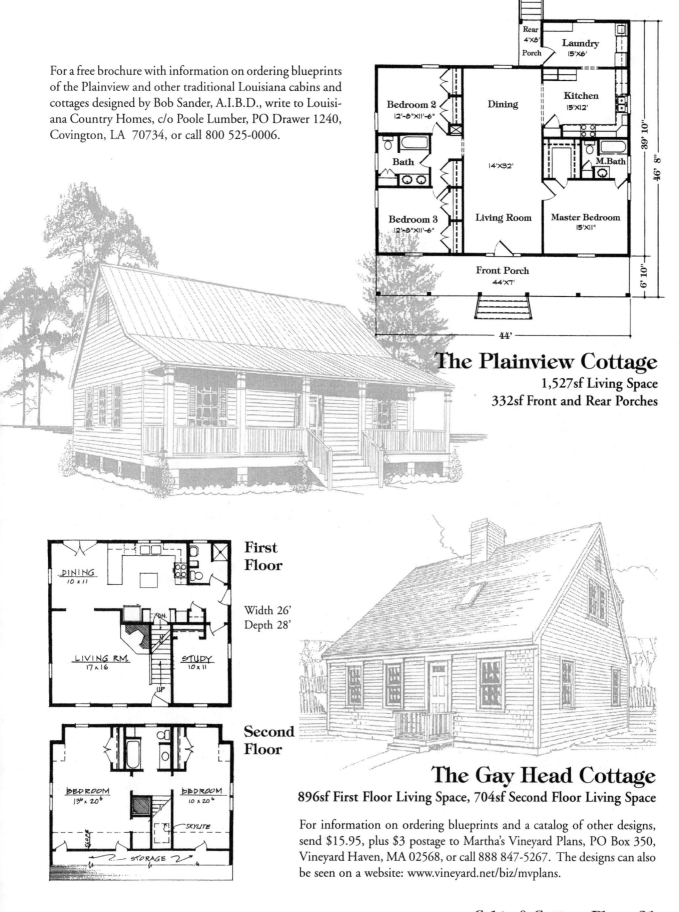

The Plainview Cottage
1,527sf Living Space
332sf Front and Rear Porches

The Gay Head Cottage
896sf First Floor Living Space, 704sf Second Floor Living Space

For information on ordering blueprints and a catalog of other designs, send $15.95, plus $3 postage to Martha's Vineyard Plans, PO Box 350, Vineyard Haven, MA 02568, or call 888 847-5267. The designs can also be seen on a website: www.vineyard.net/biz/mvplans.

The Grace Palmer House
735sf First Floor Living Space
735sf Second Floor Living Space

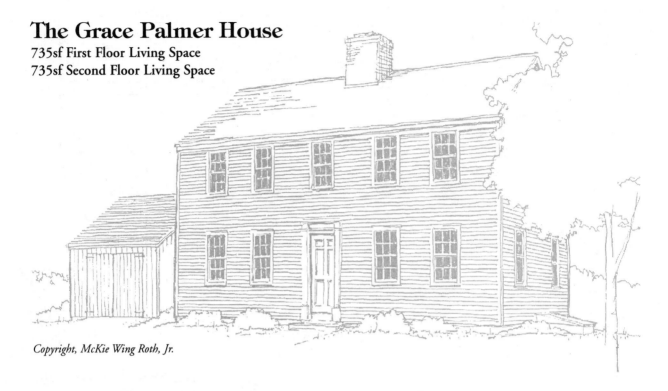

Copyright, McKie Wing Roth, Jr.

The Grace Palmer House, by McKie Roth, seems to be inspired by the vernacular "I-Houses" that dot the countryside from coast to coast. Actually, it's a new design, inspired by the same ideas. The old I-Houses were popular because they were easy to build, with narrow spans front to back, and walls that aligned on both floors. Roth created this design as a spare-time project. He's building it himself, without help, so he planned it for the simplest construction methods.

Any home is a daunting do-it-yourself project, but the ideas that make this home feasible as a one-person project make it simpler and less expensive for a professional crew.

To learn more about the Grace Palmer House and dozens of other designs, send $18.00 for the catalog *New England Style Home Designs*. It's available from McKie Roth Design, Inc. PO Box 31, Castine, ME 04421. To order by phone, call 800 232-7684. Or visit the website: www.mckieroth.com.

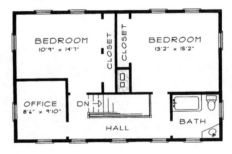

Second Floor

First Floor

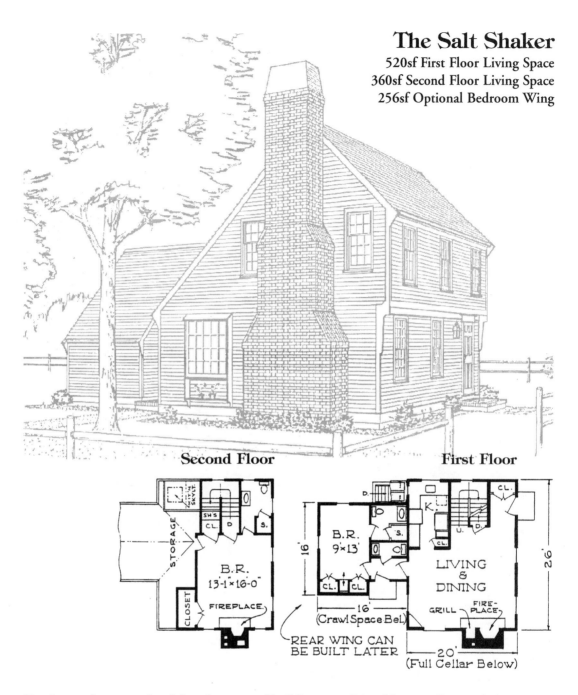

The Salt Shaker

520sf First Floor Living Space
360sf Second Floor Living Space
256sf Optional Bedroom Wing

Second Floor

First Floor

Here's a perfect example of the advantage of building a traditional home. Connecticut engineer Harry Townsend, of Eli Townsend & Son, designed his Salt Shaker house in 1972, using elements of historic New England and Tidewater homes. Now, three decades later, the design is just as attractive and appropriate as it was then. Take a trip to your library, and look at some home and architecture magazines from the early '70s. Very few designs have aged as well. Fashions change, but the house you build should last for the next few hundred years. Build something that your great-grandchildren will be proud of.

For information on construction plans for the Salt Shaker and other traditional designs, visit the website: http://albino.com/townsend. Or write for free literature to Eli Townsend & Son, 132 Hemlock Drive, Deep River, CT 06417.

Old Fire Room House

792sf First Floor Living Space
594sf Second Floor Living Space
60sf Porch

The one room, or "fire room" house, was often the first phase of construction of a home that would grow with prosperity and a family's needs. This design is a reproduction of an early 1700s home in Lincoln, Rhode Island, by architect Russell Swinton Oatman. It has an updated interior and a kitchen added in the way original homes of the time would be expanded. Like the original, this new home is small, efficient, inexpensive to heat and easy to maintain.

This is one of 18 designs in *The Cape Cod Collection of House Designs.* The catalog is available for $8.00 from Russell Swinton Oatman Design Associates, Inc., 132 Mirick Road, Princeton, MA 01541.

First Floor

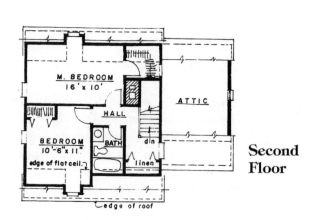

Second Floor

The Balsam Ridge Cabin

1,060sf First Floor Living Space, 552sf Second Floor Living Space
464sf Front and Rear Porches

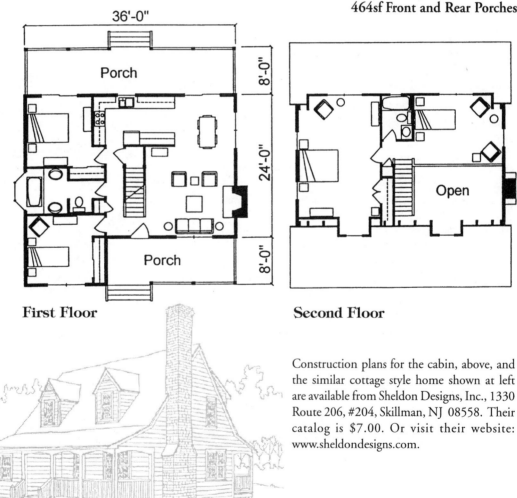

First Floor

Second Floor

Construction plans for the cabin, above, and the similar cottage style home shown at left are available from Sheldon Designs, Inc., 1330 Route 206, #204, Skillman, NJ 08558. Their catalog is $7.00. Or visit their website: www.sheldondesigns.com.

Small Bracketed Cottage
752sf First Floor Living Space
752sf Second Floor Living Space

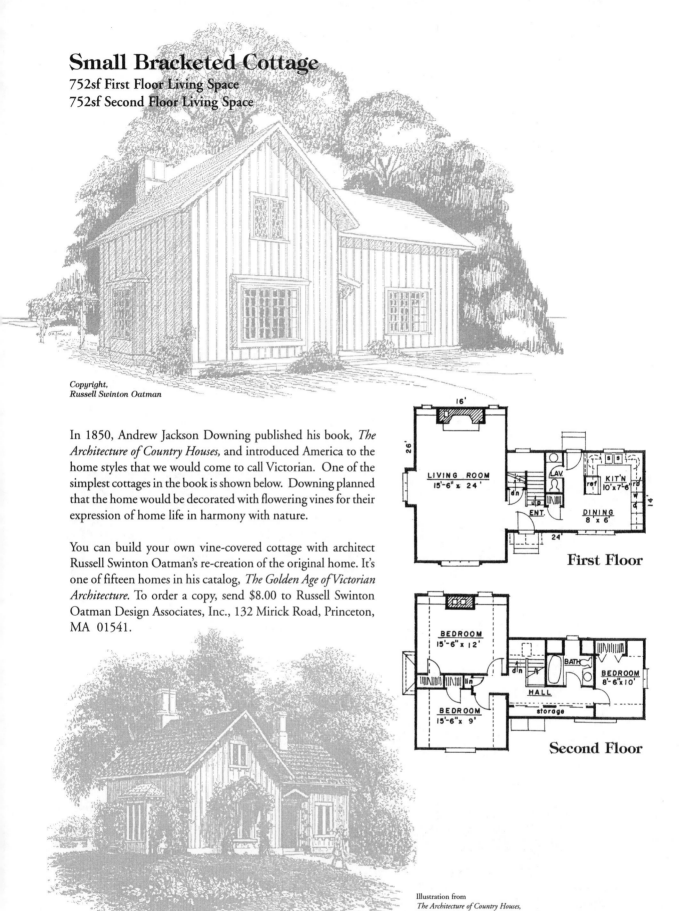

Copyright,
Russell Swinton Oatman

In 1850, Andrew Jackson Downing published his book, *The Architecture of Country Houses,* and introduced America to the home styles that we would come to call Victorian. One of the simplest cottages in the book is shown below. Downing planned that the home would be decorated with flowering vines for their expression of home life in harmony with nature.

You can build your own vine-covered cottage with architect Russell Swinton Oatman's re-creation of the original home. It's one of fifteen homes in his catalog, *The Golden Age of Victorian Architecture.* To order a copy, send $8.00 to Russell Swinton Oatman Design Associates, Inc., 132 Mirick Road, Princeton, MA 01541.

First Floor

LIVING ROOM
15'-6" x 24'

LAV.

KIT'N
10'x 7'-6

ENT.

DINING
8' x 6'

Second Floor

BEDROOM
15'-6" x 12'

BATH

BEDROOM
8'-6" x 10'

HALL

BEDROOM
15'-6" x 9'

storage

Illustration from
The Architecture of Country Houses,
1850

Cottage at Tabernacle

540sf First Floor Living Space
540sf Second Floor Living Space
186sf Porch and Balcony

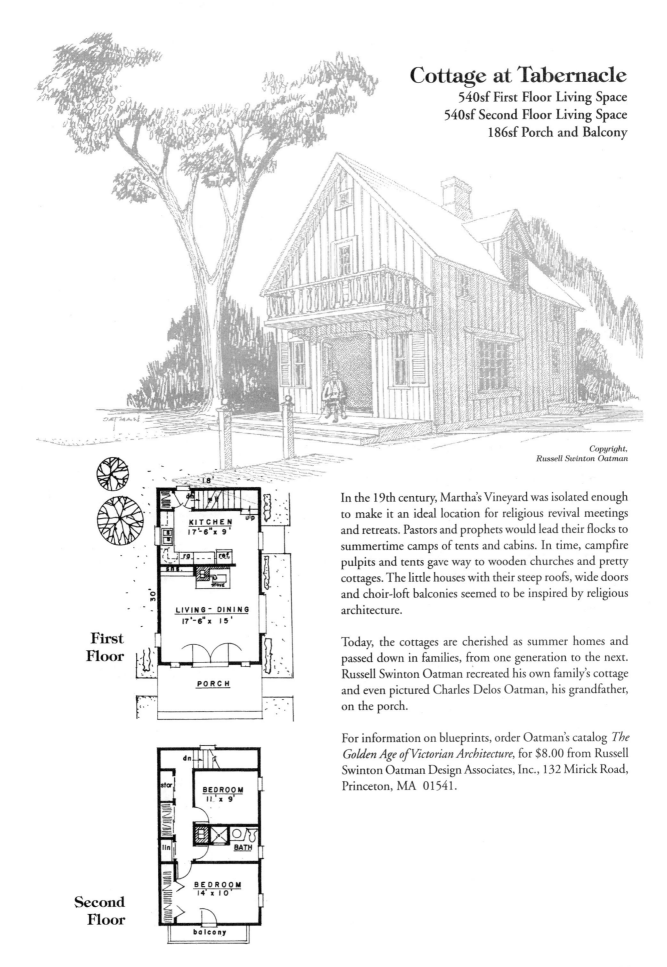

Copyright,
Russell Swinton Oatman

First Floor

Second Floor

In the 19th century, Martha's Vineyard was isolated enough to make it an ideal location for religious revival meetings and retreats. Pastors and prophets would lead their flocks to summertime camps of tents and cabins. In time, campfire pulpits and tents gave way to wooden churches and pretty cottages. The little houses with their steep roofs, wide doors and choir-loft balconies seemed to be inspired by religious architecture.

Today, the cottages are cherished as summer homes and passed down in families, from one generation to the next. Russell Swinton Oatman recreated his own family's cottage and even pictured Charles Delos Oatman, his grandfather, on the porch.

For information on blueprints, order Oatman's catalog *The Golden Age of Victorian Architecture*, for $8.00 from Russell Swinton Oatman Design Associates, Inc., 132 Mirick Road, Princeton, MA 01541.

The Chesapeake

900sf First Floor Living Space
564sf Optional Second Floor Living Space
108sf Porch

The Chesapeake is a creative adaptation of a classic Cape Cod cottage. The nontraditional front porch makes an inviting entry and a comfortable outdoor space. Like most Capes, this home can be built as a one bedroom, one floor home with an unfinished attic or as a complete three bedroom home.

For information on construction plans, order the *Homestead Design Planbook*, for $5.00 from Homestead Design, PO Box 2010, Port Townsend, WA 98368. Visit Homestead Design's website: www.homesteaddesign.com.

First Floor Plan

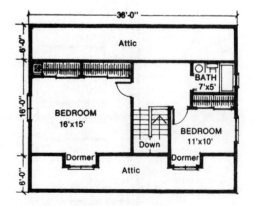

Second Floor Plan

The Kingston

768sf First Floor Living Space
768sf Second Floor Living Space
160sf Porch

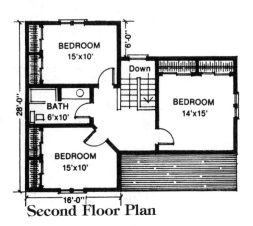

First Floor Plan

For information on blueprints for the Kingston and on other home designs, order the *Homestead Design Planbook*, for $5.00 from Homestead Design, PO Box 2010, Port Townsend, WA 98368.

Second Floor Plan

The New Castle

1,685sf First Floor Living Space
1,362sf Second Floor Expansion Area
313sf Front and Back Porches
535sf Carport and Outdoor Storage

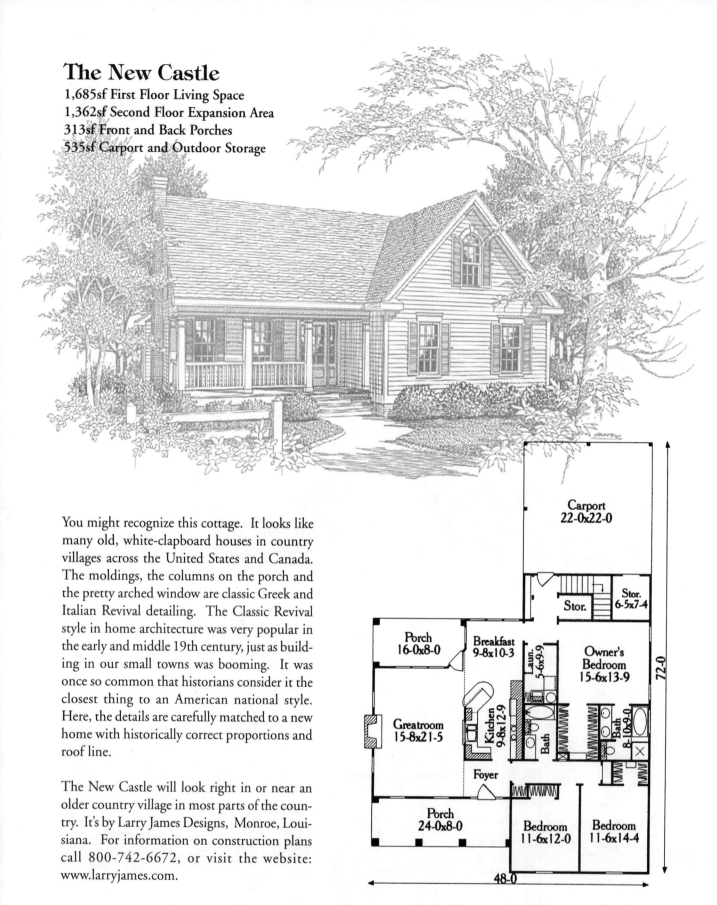

You might recognize this cottage. It looks like many old, white-clapboard houses in country villages across the United States and Canada. The moldings, the columns on the porch and the pretty arched window are classic Greek and Italian Revival detailing. The Classic Revival style in home architecture was very popular in the early and middle 19th century, just as building in our small towns was booming. It was once so common that historians consider it the closest thing to an American national style. Here, the details are carefully matched to a new home with historically correct proportions and roof line.

The New Castle will look right in or near an older country village in most parts of the country. It's by Larry James Designs, Monroe, Louisiana. For information on construction plans call 800-742-6672, or visit the website: www.larryjames.com.

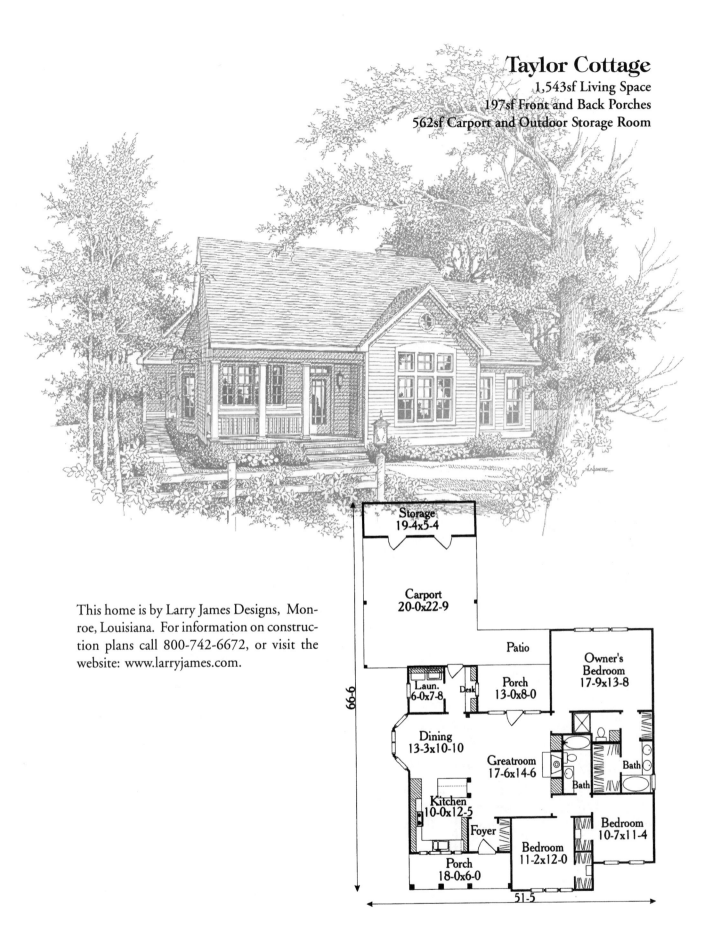

Taylor Cottage

1,543sf Living Space
197sf Front and Back Porches
562sf Carport and Outdoor Storage Room

This home is by Larry James Designs, Monroe, Louisiana. For information on construction plans call 800-742-6672, or visit the website: www.larryjames.com.

Storage
19-4x5-4

Carport
20-0x22-9

Patio

Porch
13-0x8-0

Owner's
Bedroom
17-9x13-8

Laun.
6-0x7-8

Desk

Dining
13-3x10-10

Greatroom
17-6x14-6

Bath

Bath

Kitchen
10-0x12-5

Bedroom
10-7x11-4

Foyer

Bedroom
11-2x12-0

Porch
18-0x6-0

66-9

51-5

George Ward House

1,008sf First Floor Living Space
708sf Second Floor Living Space

First Floor

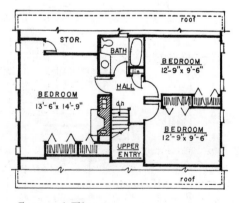

Second Floor

The George Ward House is a reproduction of a Lakeville, Massachusetts original built in 1712. Architect Russell Swinton Oatman recreated 22 historic New England homes from the 17th, 18th and 19th centuries and prepared construction drawings for use today. For complete information, order his planbook, *The New England Collection of House Designs*, for $8.00. It's available from Russell Swinton Oatman Design Associates, Inc., 132 Mirick Road, Princeton, MA 01541.

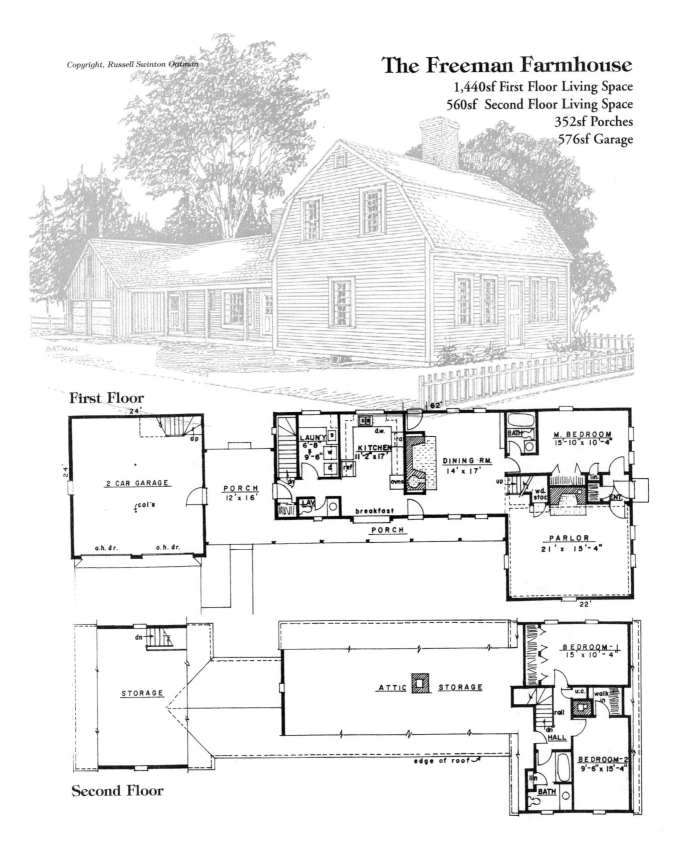

The Freeman Farmhouse

1,440sf First Floor Living Space
560sf Second Floor Living Space
352sf Porches
576sf Garage

Copyright, Russell Swinton Oatman

First Floor

2 CAR GARAGE

PORCH 12' x 16'

LAUN'Y 6'-8" 9'-6"

KITCHEN 11'-2'x17'

DINING RM. 14' x 17'

BATH

M. BEDROOM 15'-10" x 10'-4"

breakfast

PORCH

PARLOR 21' x 15'-4"

o.h.dr.   o.h.dr.

Second Floor

STORAGE

ATTIC STORAGE

edge of roof

BEDROOM-1 15' x 10'-4"

walk in

HALL

BEDROOM-2 9'-6"x 15'-4"

BATH

Looking for a farmhouse design? Here's the real thing. The Pliny Freeman farmhouse was built in Sturbridge, Massachusetts in 1802. It was moved and restored, and is now among the many early 19th century buildings on display at the Old Sturbridge Village Museum. It's also one of the museum's houses that have been carefully recreated in new plans by architect Russell Oatman. His catalog, *The Old Sturbridge Village Collection of House Designs,* is available for $7.00 from Russell Swinton Oatman Design Associates, Inc., 132 Mirick Road, Princeton, MA 01541.

Charlotte Corbin's Cottage

1737sf Living Space
405sf Front and Rear Porches

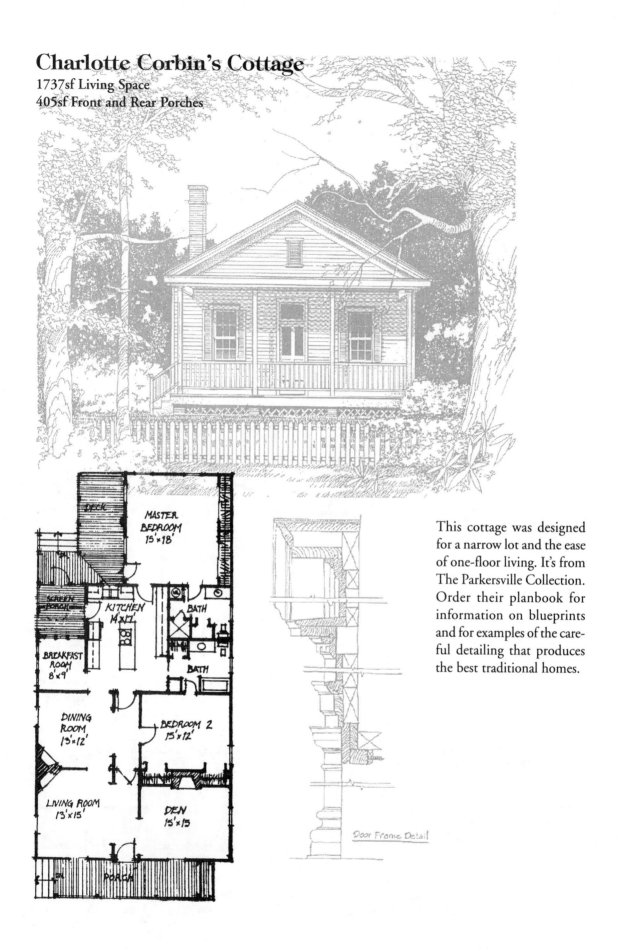

This cottage was designed for a narrow lot and the ease of one-floor living. It's from The Parkersville Collection. Order their planbook for information on blueprints and for examples of the careful detailing that produces the best traditional homes.

The William Leigh House

1,406sf First Floor Living Space
742sf Second Floor Living Space
275sf Porch

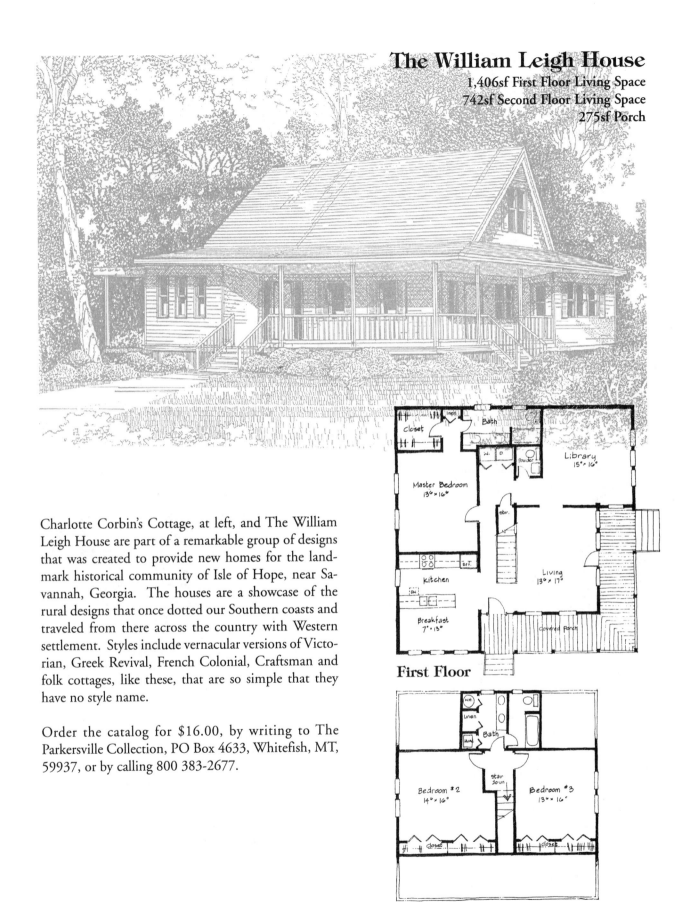

First Floor

Second Floor

Charlotte Corbin's Cottage, at left, and The William Leigh House are part of a remarkable group of designs that was created to provide new homes for the landmark historical community of Isle of Hope, near Savannah, Georgia. The houses are a showcase of the rural designs that once dotted our Southern coasts and traveled from there across the country with Western settlement. Styles include vernacular versions of Victorian, Greek Revival, French Colonial, Craftsman and folk cottages, like these, that are so simple that they have no style name.

Order the catalog for $16.00, by writing to The Parkersville Collection, PO Box 4633, Whitefish, MT, 59937, or by calling 800 383-2677.

Birkcreek Cottage
1,339sf First Floor Living Space
823sf Second Floor Living Space
1,132sf Porch
644sf Garage and Outdoor Storage

Porches were often important parts of traditional American country homes. They were summertime living rooms and summer kitchens for farmhouses. They are where folks would sit to nod and smile at passersby and chat a bit. Even today, a front porch always makes a home seem welcoming. It's a wood and shingle nod and smile.

Here's a great old-fashioned porch on a new home design. It wraps around the house and almost doubles the first floor living space.

The Birkcreek is one of 62 country designs in the *New Beginnings* catalog, available for $10.00 from Larry James Designs, 2208 Justice Street, Monroe, LA 71201, or by calling 800 742-6672. More homes are presented on a web site: www.larryjames.com.

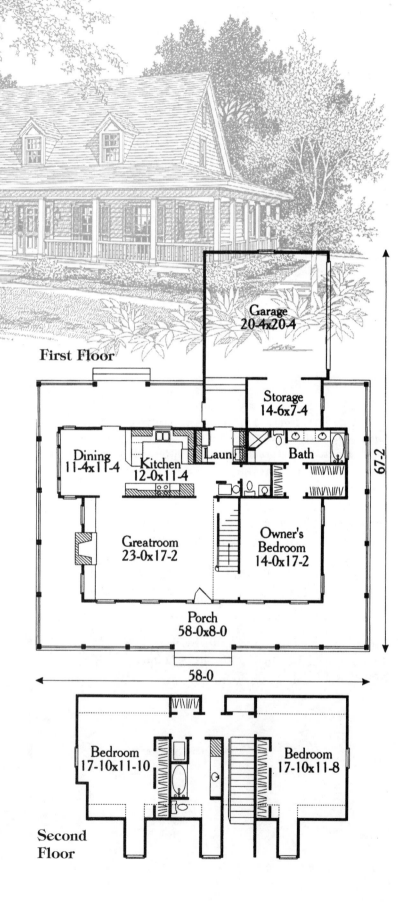

First Floor

Garage
20-4x20-4

Storage
14-6x7-4

Dining
11-4x11-4

Kitchen
12-0x11-4

Laun.

Bath

Greatroom
23-0x17-2

Owner's
Bedroom
14-0x17-2

Porch
58-0x8-0

67-2

58-0

Second Floor

Bedroom
17-10x11-10

Bedroom
17-10x11-8

Annisquam Salt Box

1,080sf First Floor Living Space
880sf Second Floor Living Space

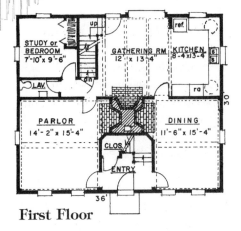

Copyright,
Russell Swinton Oatman

The New England Saltbox house design evolved in direct response to the weather. The long, low roof protected the house from cold north winds. The multi-windowed front usually faced the south and let the sun in. A massive central chimney, warmed by multiple fireplaces and ovens, would hold the heat through winter nights. Today's best passive solar homes are just variations on this design. Few look as good.

This reproduction of an 1680 original is by architect Russell Swinton Oatman. For information on construction plans, order *The New England Collection of House Designs*, for $8.00 from Russell Swinton Oatman Design Associates, Inc., 132 Mirick Road, Princeton, MA 01541.

First Floor

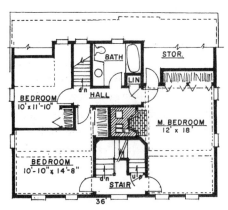

Second Floor

The Pine Island Cottage

1,188 First Floor Living Space
609sf Second Floor Living Space
360sf Front, Rear and Side Porches

Planning on working at home? Here's a Southern country house with a convenient small wing for a home office or studio.

Designer Bob Sander, A.I.B.D. has created dozens of modern homes with the simple grace and common-sense details of old Louisiana Acadian cottages. For a free catalog of his designs, write to Louisiana Country Homes, c/o Poole Lumber, PO Drawer 1240, Covington, LA 70734, or call 800 525-0006.

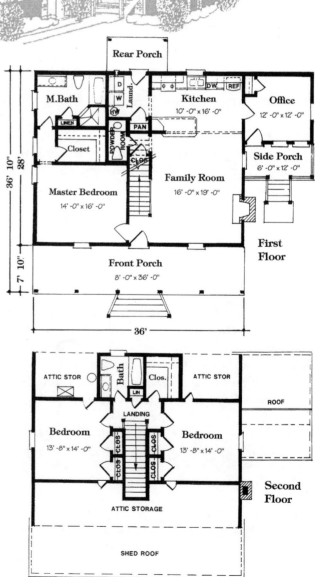

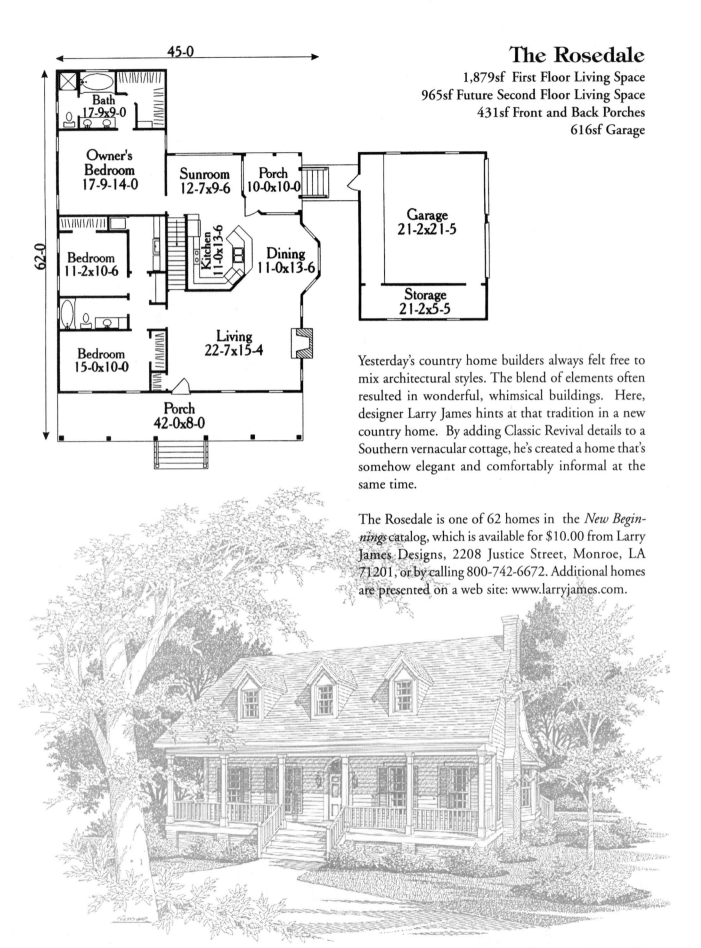

The Rosedale

1,879sf First Floor Living Space
965sf Future Second Floor Living Space
431sf Front and Back Porches
616sf Garage

45-0

62-0

Bath
17-9x9-0

Owner's
Bedroom
17-9-14-0

Sunroom
12-7x9-6

Porch
10-0x10-0

Garage
21-2x21-5

Bedroom
11-2x10-6

Kitchen
11-0x13-6

Dining
11-0x13-6

Storage
21-2x5-5

Bedroom
15-0x10-0

Living
22-7x15-4

Porch
42-0x8-0

Yesterday's country home builders always felt free to mix architectural styles. The blend of elements often resulted in wonderful, whimsical buildings. Here, designer Larry James hints at that tradition in a new country home. By adding Classic Revival details to a Southern vernacular cottage, he's created a home that's somehow elegant and comfortably informal at the same time.

The Rosedale is one of 62 homes in the *New Beginnings* catalog, which is available for $10.00 from Larry James Designs, 2208 Justice Street, Monroe, LA 71201, or by calling 800-742-6672. Additional homes are presented on a web site: www.larryjames.com.

The Abraham Tucker House

1,280sf First Floor Living Space
840sf Second Floor Living Space
437sf Garage

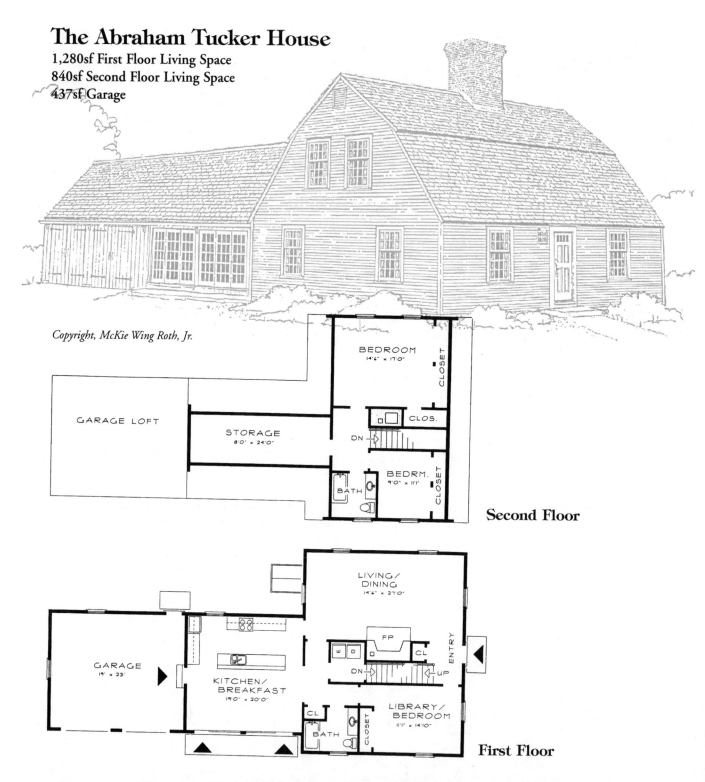

Copyright, McKie Wing Roth, Jr.

Second Floor

GARAGE LOFT

STORAGE
8'0" x 24'0"

BEDROOM
14'6" x 17'0"

CLOSET

CLOS.

DN

BATH

BEDRM.
9'0" x 11'1"

CLOSET

First Floor

GARAGE
19' x 23'

KITCHEN/
BREAKFAST
19'0" x 20'0"

LIVING/
DINING
14'6" x 27'0"

FP

W D

CL

ENTRY

DN

UP

LIBRARY/
BEDROOM
11'1" x 14'10"

CL

BATH

CLOSET

Maine designer McKie Roth created this house to withstand harsh New England winters. Like the connected farmsteads that are typical of his region, the garage is designed as a part of the home. The garage doors and big windows in the kitchen face south to capture the warmth of the sun. An insulated gambrel roof blankets the home, and the north side has less glass.

For information on construction plans, order the catalog *New England Style Home Designs,* for $18.00 from McKie Roth Design, Inc., PO Box 31, Castine, ME 04421, call 800 232-7684, or visit the website: www.mckieroth.com.

The Classic Screen Porch

You'll need more than a good home plan to build the perfect country place. The next chapter presents catalogs that feature plans of classic country backbuildings: barns, stables, garages and sheds. There are also dozens of other little structures that can improve your enjoyment of your country property. An outdoor shower will help keep sand and mud where they belong. It's a great way to cool off after weeding the hot summer garden. A screen porch lets you enjoy the outdoors in rain or shine. It expands the space of your home at a fraction of the cost of a heated room.

The Classic Screen Porch above, is 14' x 24,' and features a timber frame structure and roof trusses. The Lattice Shower is 5' x 9', with a built-in bench. The exterior is a trellis for roses or climbing vines.

Do you need a deck, fences, a trash bin or a dog house? You'll find blueprints and inspiration in the catalog from Martha's Vineyard Plans, PO Box 350, Vineyard Haven, MA 02568. Order it by mail for $15.95 plus $3 postage, or call 888 847-5267. Their website is: www.vineyard.net/biz/mvplans.

The Lattice Shower

Just Outbuildings

Garden sheds, garages, studios, pool houses and a gazebo - just outbuildings and just terrific designs. There are 18 designs presented, all with architect's blueprints available at reasonable prices. This Country Garage has a full loft with a convenient lift-post and hatch. A catalog is available for $5.00, from Just Outbuildings, PO Box 42, Brewster, NY, 10509.

McKie Roth Design

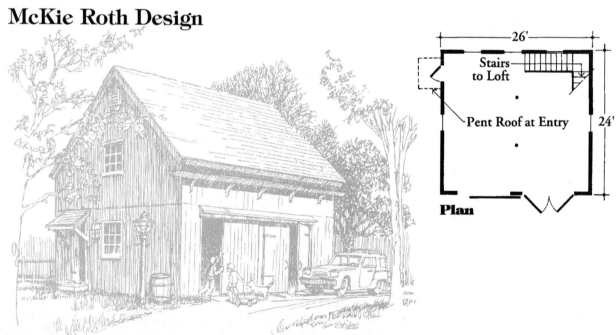

Besides the Cape Cods, Saltboxes, Farmhouses and Georgian style homes in McKie Roth's catalog of study plans, you'll find backyard barns designed to complement them. The Stockbridge Buggy Barn, shown here, is a two bay garage with a full loft above. Roth's catalog is available for $18.00 from McKie Roth Design, Inc., PO Box 31, Castine, ME 04421. Or call 800 232-7684.

10'-6" — **14'**

8'

Stairs to Loft

Garage & Shop

13'

Plan

Backbuildings

No country place is finished without a backbuilding or two. You'll need a garage for the cars, a garden shed for the yard tools and, perhaps, a stable or workshop. Or you can build a big barn to fit everything.

The designs here and on the next few pages are just a small sampling of hundreds of building plans offered in the catalogs listed. Like the cottages and cabins in the last section, these are all shown at the same scale, 1/16" = 1'-0," so that you can quickly compare sizes.

The Country Building Directory, in this book, lists the catalogs of other plan services and builders of kits and pre-built sheds.

The book, *Barns and Backbuildings*, a companion to this volume, presents 94 traditional wooden outbuildings by eleven architects and designers. You can order inexpensive blueprints directly from the book. It has information on planning your property and sources for hard-to-find products like carriage house doors, rolling door hardware, cupolas, weather vanes, stable equipment and much more. See page 95 for ordering information.

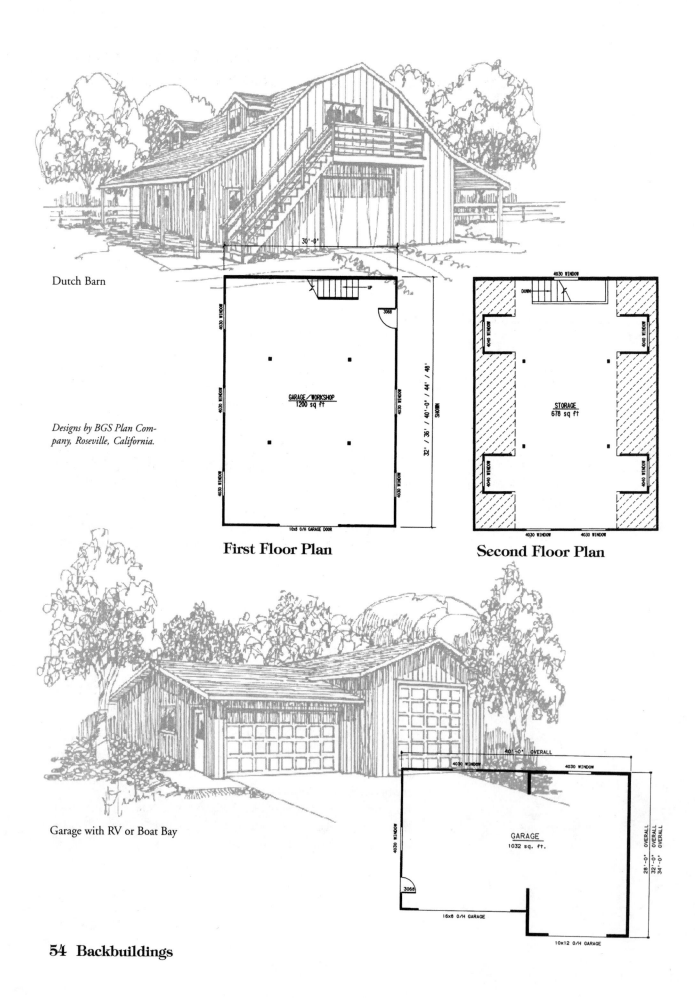

Dutch Barn

Designs by BGS Plan Company, Roseville, California.

GARAGE/WORKSHOP
1200 sq ft

10x8 O/H GARAGE DOOR

30'-0"

32' / 36' / 40'-0" / 44' / 48'
SHOWN

First Floor Plan

4030 WINDOW

DOWN

STORAGE
678 sq ft

4040 WINDOW   4040 WINDOW

4040 WINDOW   4040 WINDOW

4030 WINDOW   4030 WINDOW

Second Floor Plan

Garage with RV or Boat Bay

40'-0" OVERALL

4030 WINDOW   4030 WINDOW

GARAGE
1032 sq. ft.

3066

16x8 O/H GARAGE

10x12 O/H GARAGE

28'-0" OVERALL
32'-0" OVERALL
34'-0" OVERALL

54 Backbuildings

BGS Plan Company
Barns, Garages, Shops and Accessory Buildings

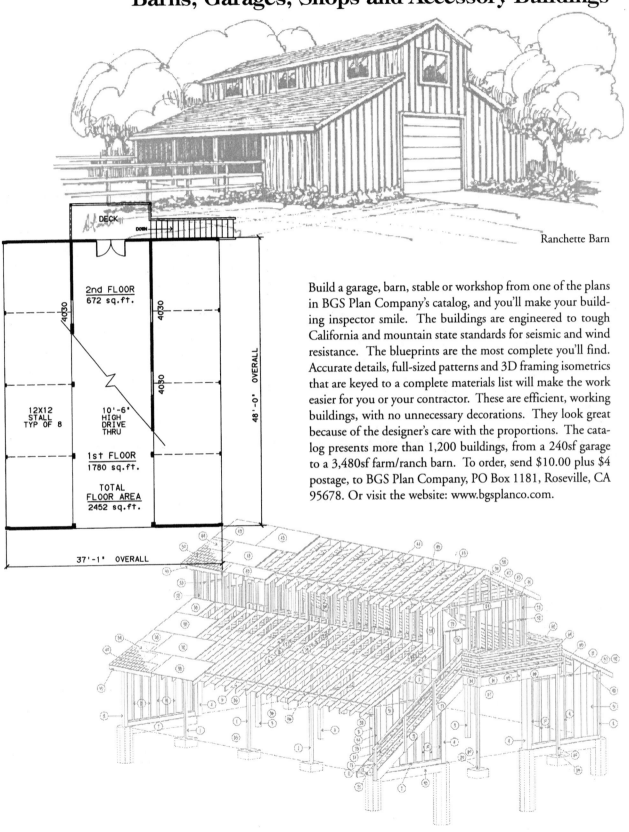

Ranchette Barn

2nd FLOOR
672 sq.ft.

4030

4030

12X12
STALL
TYP OF 8

10'-6"
HIGH
DRIVE
THRU

4030

48'-0" OVERALL

1st FLOOR
1780 sq.ft.

TOTAL
FLOOR AREA
2452 sq.ft.

DECK
DOWN

37'-1" OVERALL

Build a garage, barn, stable or workshop from one of the plans in BGS Plan Company's catalog, and you'll make your building inspector smile. The buildings are engineered to tough California and mountain state standards for seismic and wind resistance. The blueprints are the most complete you'll find. Accurate details, full-sized patterns and 3D framing isometrics that are keyed to a complete materials list will make the work easier for you or your contractor. These are efficient, working buildings, with no unnecessary decorations. They look great because of the designer's care with the proportions. The catalog presents more than 1,200 buildings, from a 240sf garage to a 3,480sf farm/ranch barn. To order, send $10.00 plus $4 postage, to BGS Plan Company, PO Box 1181, Roseville, CA 95678. Or visit the website: www.bgsplanco.com.

Sheldon Designs

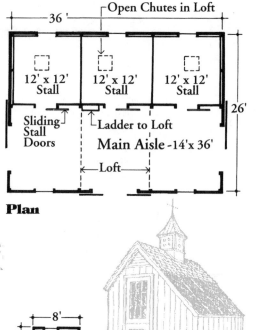

Architect Andrew Sheldon has created a collection of 55 variations of country barns, stables, garages and sheds. They range in size from the 64sf garden shed and greenhouse at right, to the 936sf pole-barn, above. Inexpensive, easy-to-read blueprints are available for all. The catalog is $7.00 from Sheldon Designs, Inc., 1330 Route 206, #204, Skillman, NJ 08558. Or visit the website: www.sheldondesigns.com.

Martha's Vineyard Plans

You'll find a creative selection of all types of backyard buildings in Martha's Vineyard Plans' catalog. It offers construction drawings for garages, decks, gazebos, porches, sheds, trash bins, guest cottages and garage apartments. The Harthaven Car Barn, shown here, is 28' deep and 38' wide. It has a loft above and three big bays below. The center bay is 10' high, with 9' doors for a boat, RV or camper. Send $15.95, plus $3 postage, for the planbook to Martha's Vineyard Plans, PO Box 350, Vineyard Haven, MA 02568, or call 888 847-5267. The designs can also be seen on a website: www.vineyard.net/biz/mvplans.

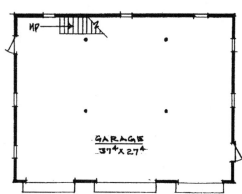

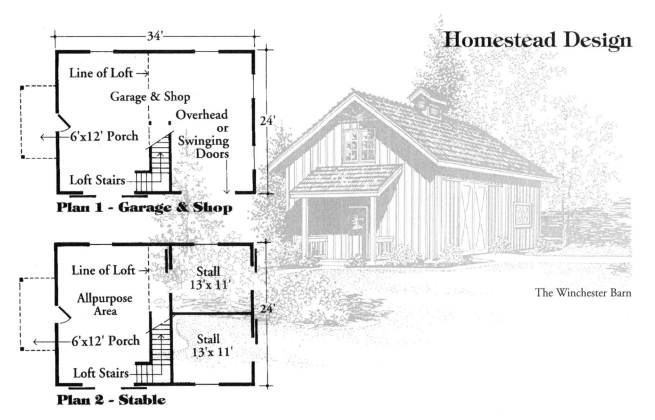

34'

Line of Loft →

Garage & Shop

24'

← 6'x12' Porch

Overhead or Swinging Doors

Loft Stairs

Plan 1 - Garage & Shop

Line of Loft →

Allpurpose Area

Stall 13'x 11'

24'

← 6'x12' Porch

Stall 13'x 11'

Loft Stairs →

Plan 2 - Stable

The Winchester Barn

Homestead Design's collection of barns, garages, stables, greenhouses and garden sheds features attractive, simple designs and clever, flexible layouts. Many of the designs are offered with two or more alternative plans, giving flexibility before and after construction. The barn above is a good example. Horse owners know that a stable doesn't add value to a property, but a garage does. This barn can be built as stable and converted easily to a two bay garage and shop. With all the variations in plans, there are more than 40 country buildings in *The Homestead Design Planbook*. It's available for $5.00 from Homestead Design, PO Box 2010, Port Townsend, WA 98368. The buildings can also be seen on Homestead's website: www.homesteaddesign.com.

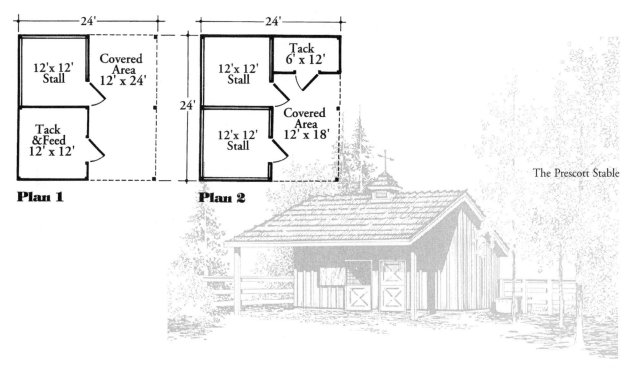

24'

12'x 12' Stall

Covered Area 12' x 24'

Tack &Feed 12' x 12'

Plan 1

24'

12'x 12' Stall

Tack 6' x 12'

24'

12'x 12' Stall

Covered Area 12' x 18'

Plan 2

The Prescott Stable

Country Designs

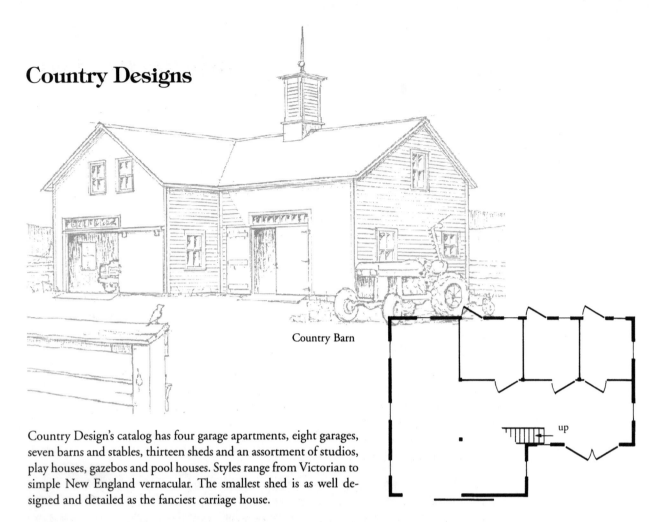

Country Barn

Country Design's catalog has four garage apartments, eight garages, seven barns and stables, thirteen sheds and an assortment of studios, play houses, gazebos and pool houses. Styles range from Victorian to simple New England vernacular. The smallest shed is as well designed and detailed as the fanciest carriage house.

The Country Barn, above, is 22' x 30,' with a 20' x 22' wing and a full loft. The stalls shown are optional, so the barn can serve any use. The Coach House is a 22' x 26,' two car garage and shop, with a full apartment on the second floor.

For information on blueprints, and to see the other designs, order the catalog for $8.00 from Country Designs, PO Box 774, Essex, CT 06426.

Coach House

First Floor

Garage

Second Floor

LR/K

BR

Backyard Pole Barns

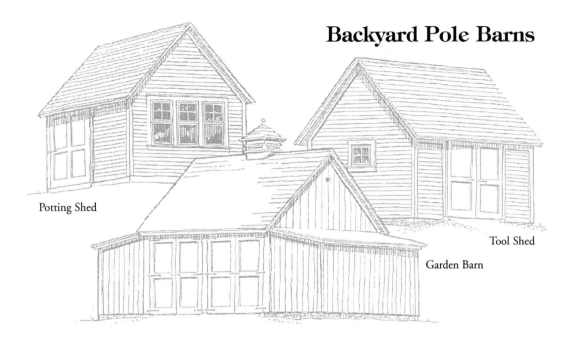

Potting Shed

Tool Shed

Garden Barn

Farmers know that the simplest and least expensive way to build is by pole framing. With pole barns, a series of wooden posts are set into small post holes. Then the walls and roof are hung from the posts. It's a lot like building a fence. The huge ditches and formwork for conventional foundations aren't necessary. The cost savings comes from less site work and less concrete. Most pole framed buildings cost 25% less than conventional buildings of the same size.

You don't have to build a big farm barn to take advantage of pole framing. If you need a garden shed, garage, backyard barn or workshop, dozens of inexpensive pole frame construction plans are available. The sheds shown above are all based on a 10' x 14' floor plan and supported by 4x4 pressure-treated posts. They make fine do-it-yourself projects and are a good introduction to pole framing. The Candlewood Barn, below, is a combination one bay garage, workshop and tractor shed. It has a full loft with pull-down stairs and an access hatch. Other barns range up in size to six parking bays. All are designed as traditional country backbuildings. Order the brochure, *Backyard Barns,* by sending $3.00 to Donald J. Berg, AIA, PO Box 698, Rockville Centre, NY 11571.

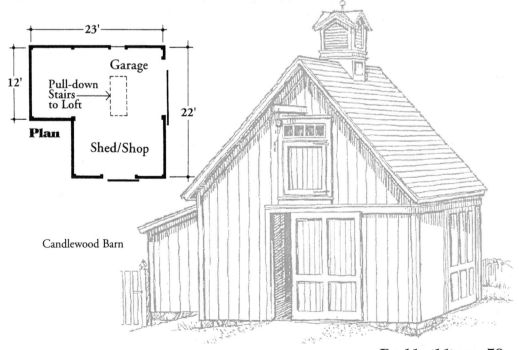

Candlewood Barn

Country Building Kits

24,' One Story Country Barn.
Available in 24' x 24,' 24' x 30,'
24' x 36,' 24' x 48' and 24' x 60'

Horse Barn, Shop or Garage
Not to Scale

Designs copyright, Country Carpenters

Kits are a great way of building in the country. All of the lumber is shipped to your site, pre-cut and marked for easy assembly. Because there's little wasted wood and because the buildings are designed to go together easily, you can usually have a top quality building at a reasonable price. Look in the Country Building Directory for cabin, shed and barn kit builders.

The designs on this page are samples of the dozens of post-and-beam designs available from Country Carpenters, of Hebron, Connecticut. They build their barns, sheds, stables and carriage houses in central New England. Anywhere else, they'll ship a pre-cut kit, with instructions on how you or your builder can put them together. For a copy of their catalog, send $4.00 to Country Carpenters, 326 Gilead Street, Hebron, CT 06248. Or see the designs on their website: www.countrycarpenters.com

Garden sheds are available in six sizes from 9' x 11' to 12' x 19'

Garage, Workshop or Stable
Not to Scale

One and One Half Story Barn - 22' wide x 30' shown. Also available in 18' and 24' widths, and a variety of lengths.

Other Sources
of
Backroad Designs

Order all of the plan books and visit all of the websites listed with the cabin, cottage and backbuilding designs in this book, and you'll see over 1,700 different country buildings. Still can't find one that's just right? Don't give up. You'll see dozens of other plan books listed in the Country Building Directory, in the next chapter. And plan books aren't the only source of great country designs. On the next few pages, you'll find some more ideas.

Magazine Plans

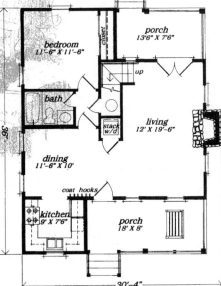

Deer Run Cabin, by William Phillips, AIA, from the *Southern Living Cabin Collection*

Copyright, Southern Living House Plans

First Floor (not to scale)

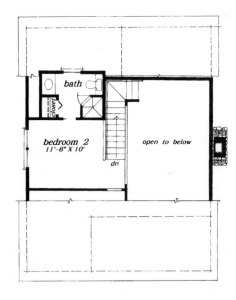

Second Floor (not to scale)

A few magazines offer blueprints of timeless homes in traditional country styles. Order their plan books or special issues for dozens of designs.

The Old House Journal publishes their special *Historic House Plans* issue twice each year. Although the focus is on high-style period homes, a number of small and simple country cottages and outbuildings are always included. The issues include informative articles and a directory of reproduction building fixtures and materials. You'll find the latest issue on newsstands, or call 800 931-2931.

Better Homes and Gardens publishes its *Country House Plans* four times each year. Every issue features some small cabins, cottages and bungalows. Articles highlight new, custom-designed country homes that are now available as stock plans. You'll find it on newsstands, or call 800 867-8628.

Country Living magazine's *Country Living Dream Homes* has two issues a year. The latest issue had a section on cottages and bungalows, one on seaside retreats and another on country outbuildings. Call 800 925-0485, or check your newsstand.

Southern Living magazine produces a series of plan books with homes in traditional Southern styles. The homes can be seen on a website: www.southernliving.com/hp. If you enjoy the cabins and cottages in this book, you'll love the *Southern Living Cabin Collection*, with designs by Alabama architect William Phillips, AIA. The sixteen little homes include a classic "dogtrot" cabin and designs inspired by vernacular houses, a mill, a country church, a Carpenter Gothic cottage and a country store. The portfolio is available for $20.00 from Southern Living House Plans, 2100 Lakeshore Drive, Birmingham, AL 35209, or call 800 755-1122.

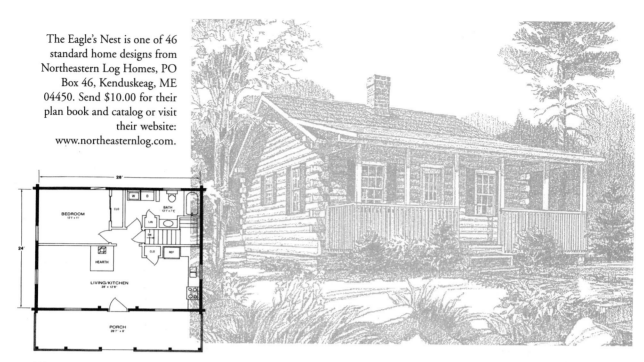

The Eagle's Nest is one of 46 standard home designs from Northeastern Log Homes, PO Box 46, Kenduskeag, ME 04450. Send $10.00 for their plan book and catalog or visit their website: www.northeasternlog.com.

Plan (not to scale)

Log Home Plans

Log cabins are America's symbol of country living. Today's log homes are nothing like the drafty, rough and rotting backwoods cabins of the past. Modern engineering and manufacturing methods make tight, long lasting homes.

There are dozens of log home manufacturers who offer both standard plans and custom designs. They'll provide a complete kit of the shell of a home and connect you with an experienced local builder for help putting it together. In addition, hundreds of other log builders will "hand craft" a home, or build it on site, from their own portfolios of plans.

Look through the Country Building Directory for a sampling of the offerings by log home manufacturers and builders. Beyond that, there is an enormous amount of easily available information on log home designs.

Three magazines publish home plans on a regular basis. You'll find them all on newsstands. *Country's Best Log Homes* has a feature on floor plans in each issue. Call 703 471-2041 for information on subscribing. *Log Homes Illustrated* includes its "Showcase of Plans" feature in each issue. In addition, they publish a special issue, called *Log Home Plans*, twice each year. Write for subscription information to *Log Homes Illustrated*, PO Box 612, Mount Morris, IL 61054-7604. *Log Home Living* features its "Focus on Floorplans" in each monthly issue and has an annual floorplans issue. For information on subscriptions and back issues, call 800 234-8496, or visit the website: www.loghomeliving.com.

There are two major log home builder trade associations. The Log Builders Association has a free information packet on hand crafted log homes. Write to them at PO Box 28608, Bellingham, WA 98228-0608, call 360 752-1303, or visit their

Log Home Plans

(Continued)

website: www.logassociation.com. The Log Home Council of the National Association of Home Builders provides information on home manufacturers. They offer a free brochure on log home living and a directory of their members. Call them at 800 368-5242, or write to 15th & M Streets, Washington, DC 20005.

On-line magazines offer log building books, products, directories and links to manufacturers' and builders' websites. Visit *LogHome.Net:* www.loghome.net, *Log Homes Net Zine:* www.ksmenet.com/netzine/, and *The Log Home Show:* www.loghomeshow.com.

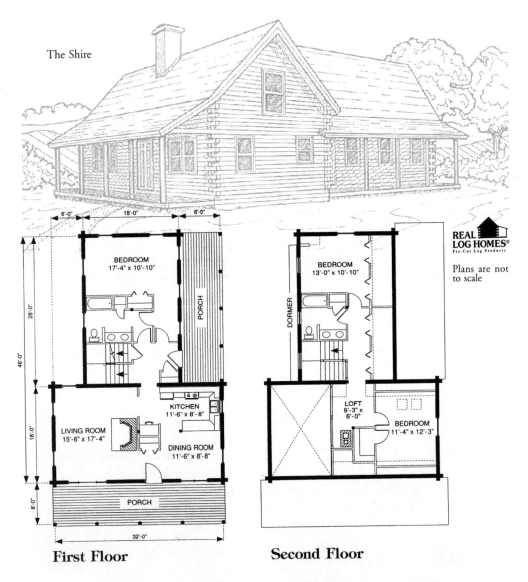

The Shire

REAL LOG HOMES®
Pre-Cut Log Products

Plans are not to scale

First Floor   **Second Floor**

The Shire is one of more than 40 designs in the *Portfolio of Floor Plans,* available for $10.00 from Real Log Homes, PO Box 202, Hartland, VT 05048. Call 800 732-5564 or visit their website: www.realloghomes.com.

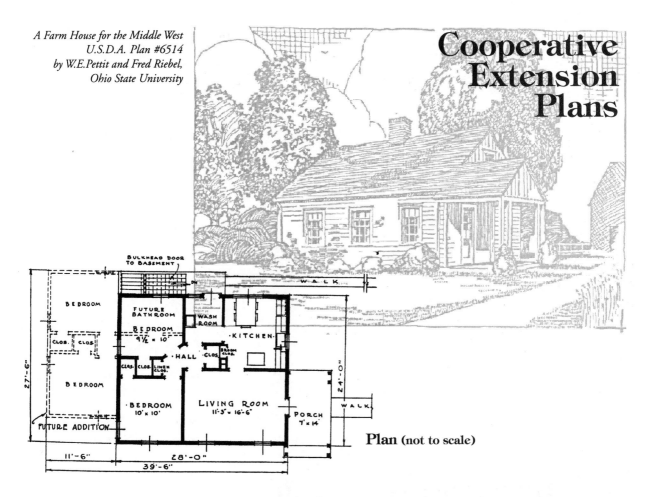

A Farm House for the Middle West
U.S.D.A. Plan #6514
by W.E.Pettit and Fred Riebel,
Ohio State University

Cooperative Extension Plans

Plan (not to scale)

Starting in the depression era, the U.S. Department of Agriculture sponsored the design and preparation of construction drawings for all types of rural buildings. Most of the work was done by architects and engineers employed by the agricultural departments of state universities. The designs are a treasure trove of well planned country buildings that reflect the characteristics of the regions that they were designed for. There are thousands of plans for barns, stables, animal shelters, grain and feed storage buildings, workshops, garages, greenhouses, farmhouses, cottages and cabins.

The individual state universities are the repositories for the drawings that their employees prepared. Many will provide blueprints of the plans at very reasonable prices. Unfortunately, most universities don't maintain catalogs of their designs, so finding a design that suits your needs can be an adventure. The best place to start is the book, *Buildings for Small Acreages*, by James S. Boyd, revised by Carl L. Reynolds (Danville, IL: Interstate Publishers, 1996). It reproduces drawings of dozens of the cabins and country structures and provides a descriptive list of other available designs and state by state addresses of the universities with Cooperative Extension Service Offices that provide the plans.

As with all published plans, these drawings should be reviewed by a qualified building professional prior to construction. Many of the older plans have to be updated to meet modern code requirements.

The Saltbox II

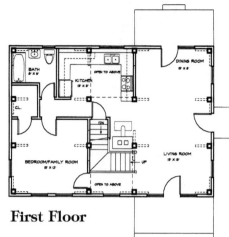

First Floor

The Saltbox II is one of the many home designs in a plan portfolio from Woodhouse -The Timber Frame Company, Box 219, Route 549, Mansfield, PA 16933. Order it for $17.00 by mail or by calling 800 227-4311.

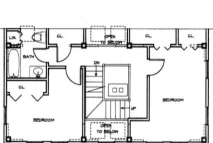

Second Floor

Timber Frame Plans

There are more than 1,000 professional timber framers in America. Many build standard home designs and publish illustrated plan books. Working on post and beam structures is an ancient craft. Most of its modern practitioners have an appreciation for traditional homes and country backbuilding, and that shows in their designs.

You'll find a small sampling of timber frame plan books listed in the Country Building Directory. Most of the timber framers who publish plan books are listed in a directory that's mailed with orders for the informative booklet, *Building a Timber Frame Home: A Client's Guide.* To order a copy, send $1.10 to the Timber Frame Business Council, PO Box B1161, Hanover, NH 03755. Their website is: www.timberframe.org.

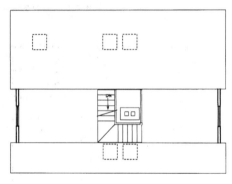

Loft   Plans are not to scale

Timber Frame Plans

(Continued)

Two magazines publish plans of timber frame homes as regular features. *Timber Frame Homes* has an article called "Focus On Floorplans," with a variety of designs in each issue. It's on newsstands, or call 800 826-3893. *Timber Homes Illustrated* publishes its "Showcase of Homes" in each issue. To subscribe, call 800 442-1869 or look for the latest issue on your newsstand.

BackHome magazine publishes just one home plan, but if you're interested in a post and beam home, it's worth ordering. Plans for their 1,700sf saltbox style house include detailed drawings of all of the timbers, clear isometric drawings of all of the mortise and tenon joints and photos of the of the finished structure. A unique work schedule for the day that the frame is raised and photos of the raising give a good introduction to the process. Order plans for The Traditional Timber Frame Saltbox by calling 800 992-2546, or by mailing $30.00 to *BackHome* Plans, PO Box 70, Hendersonville, NC 28793.

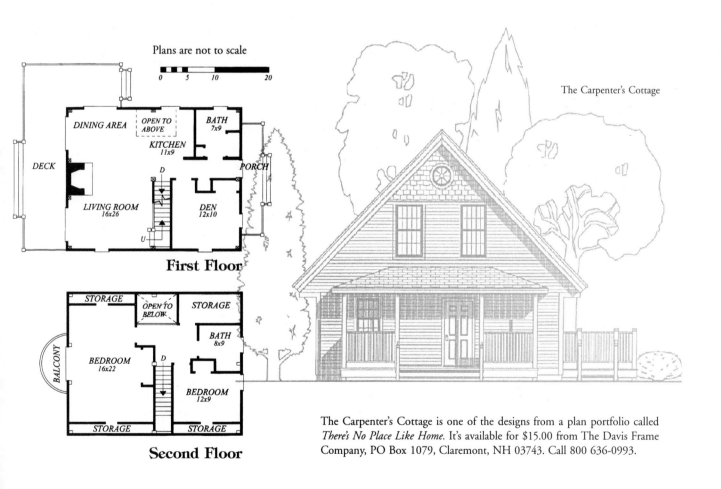

Plans are not to scale

0   5   10   20

First Floor

DECK

DINING AREA OPEN TO ABOVE BATH 7x9

KITCHEN 11x9

PORCH

LIVING ROOM 16x26 DEN 12x10

Second Floor

BALCONY

STORAGE OPEN TO BELOW STORAGE

BATH 8x9

BEDROOM 16x22

BEDROOM 12x9

STORAGE STORAGE

The Carpenter's Cottage

The Carpenter's Cottage is one of the designs from a plan portfolio called *There's No Place Like Home*. It's available for $15.00 from The Davis Frame Company, PO Box 1079, Claremont, NH 03743. Call 800 636-0993.

Historic Plans

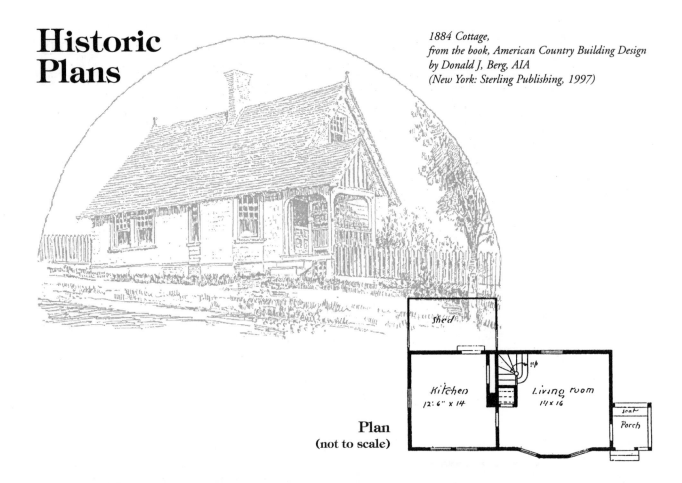

1884 Cottage,
from the book, American Country Building Design
by Donald J, Berg, AIA
(New York: Sterling Publishing, 1997)

Plan
(not to scale)

If you're looking for a traditional country building, you can find inspiration in one of the many reprints of 19th century plan books. Country cottage, cabin, carriage house and barn plans are fairly easy to re-create because the original buildings were straightforward. You'll need to work with an architect because new plans will have to be prepared. The old layouts need to be updated a bit. You'll probably want indoor plumbing. And you'll need accurate blueprints for permits, for construction estimates and to build from. The best architect is someone with experience at restoration work, who has a sensitivity for historic proportions and who is familiar with replication materials, details and fixtures.

For a large selection of 19th century home plan book reprints, write for the free *Dover Books on Architecture* catalog, to Dover Publications, Inc., 31 East 2nd Street, Mineola, NY 11501.

The classic book on 19th century barns and outbuildings is *Barns, Sheds and Outbuildings,* by Byron D. Halstead. A reprint of the 1881 original is available for $14.00 and $3.50 postage from Alan C. Hood & Company, Inc., PO Box 775, Chambersburg, PA 17201.

Custom Design

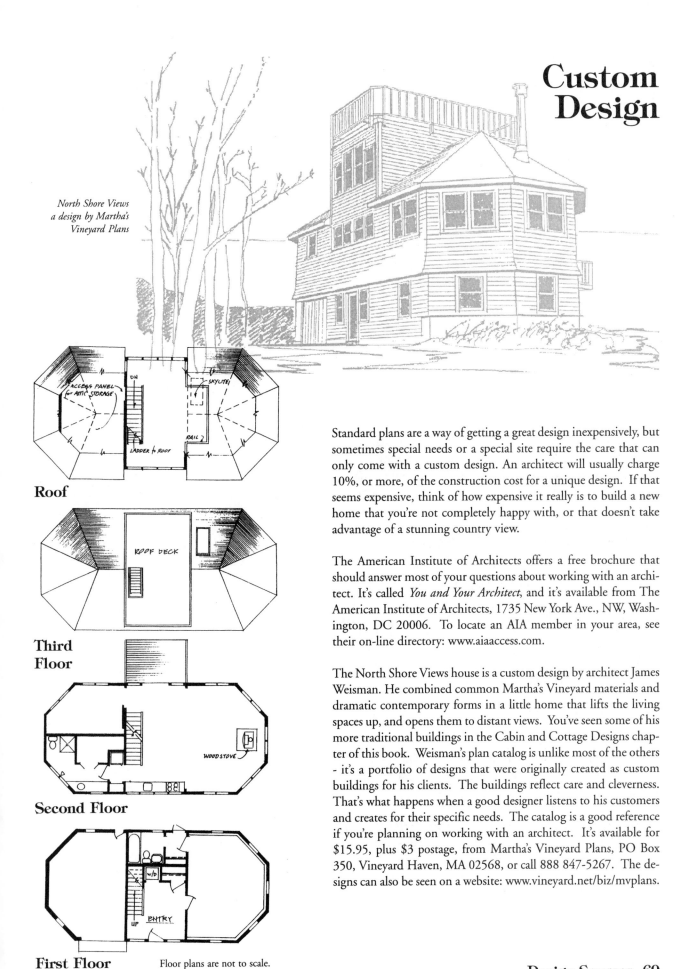

*North Shore Views
a design by Martha's
Vineyard Plans*

Roof

Third Floor

ROOF DECK

Second Floor

WOOD STOVE

First Floor   Floor plans are not to scale.

ACCESS PANEL for ATTIC STORAGE
DN
SKYLITE!
RAIL
LADDER to ROOF

w/d
UP ENTRY

Standard plans are a way of getting a great design inexpensively, but sometimes special needs or a special site require the care that can only come with a custom design. An architect will usually charge 10%, or more, of the construction cost for a unique design. If that seems expensive, think of how expensive it really is to build a new home that you're not completely happy with, or that doesn't take advantage of a stunning country view.

The American Institute of Architects offers a free brochure that should answer most of your questions about working with an architect. It's called *You and Your Architect*, and it's available from The American Institute of Architects, 1735 New York Ave., NW, Washington, DC 20006. To locate an AIA member in your area, see their on-line directory: www.aiaaccess.com.

The North Shore Views house is a custom design by architect James Weisman. He combined common Martha's Vineyard materials and dramatic contemporary forms in a little home that lifts the living spaces up, and opens them to distant views. You've seen some of his more traditional buildings in the Cabin and Cottage Designs chapter of this book. Weisman's plan catalog is unlike most of the others - it's a portfolio of designs that were originally created as custom buildings for his clients. The buildings reflect care and cleverness. That's what happens when a good designer listens to his customers and creates for their specific needs. The catalog is a good reference if you're planning on working with an architect. It's available for $15.95, plus $3 postage, from Martha's Vineyard Plans, PO Box 350, Vineyard Haven, MA 02568, or call 888 847-5267. The designs can also be seen on a website: www.vineyard.net/biz/mvplans.

Restorations

Is there a ramshackle old house or barn on your property or near it? Think of it as the heart of your new home. Look at it for what it was once and could be again. Many run-down buildings, or decent ones that stand in the way of progress, are available for the asking. Your cost comes in moving the building and renovating it. The rule of thumb is that the combined cost will be the same, or just slightly more than building new. And, you'll be preserving a piece of history.

The last page of each recent issue of *This Old House* magazine featured one historic home that's yours for the moving and $1.00. Call 800 898-7237 for subscriptions or back issues. Realtors and members of your local historical society may know of salvageable buildings in your neighborhood.

A number of specialists save falling barns and log cabins, repair the damage and resell them as the structure of new country homes. Hundred year old timber frames and cabins can cost the same or less than new frames or cabin kits. Imagine living in a pioneer's cabin. If you can find one that suits your needs, it can make the perfect backroad home. You'll find a number of sources for antique log cabins and timber frames in the Country Building Directory, on the following pages.

Also check *The Barn Journal On-line*. Charles Leik, the editor of the internet magazine, encourages readers to post information on available timber frames in free classified ads. He also maintains a state by state list of restoration specialists. Visit the website: http://museum.cl.edu/barn.

For help in the restoration process, refer to *Old-House Journal* magazine's annual *Restoration Directory*. It's on newsstands, or call 800 931-2931 to order a copy. *Traditional Building Magazine* publishes a directory of restoration products and specialists in each issue. Call 718 636-0750 to subscribe, or see the on-line directory at their website: www.traditional-building.com.

Country Building Directory

Air-Lock Log Homes

Acorn Forged Iron

457 School Street, P.O. Box 31, Mansfield, MA 02048
Decorative builders' hardware for exterior and interior doors, cabinets, gates and shutters. Catalog: $10.00. Free product literature. Phone: 800 835-0121. Fax: 800 372-2676. Website: www.acornmfg.com.
New Forged Hardware

Air-Lock Log Homes

PO Box 2506, Las Vegas, NM 87701
Founded in 1955, Air-Lock Log Homes manufactures kits with logs cut and notched to exact lengths and angles. Logs are numbered to fit to plan precisely. They serve the southwest states. Catalog: $7.00. Phone: 800 786-0525. Fax: 505 425-7636. E-mail: air-lock@air-lock.com. Website: www.air-lock.com.
Log Cabin and Home Kits, Custom Design

Allen Cupolas

2242 Bethel Road, Lansdale, PA 19446
Allen Cupolas has a complete selection of cupolas in poplar, redwood and cedar, with copper, brass or aluminum roofs. They have custom sawmill capabilities on premises. Free brochure. Phone: 610 584-8100 or phone, then Fax: 215 699-8100. E-mail: vickallen@msn.
Cupolas, Woodwork

Antique Hardware & Home

19 Buckingham Plantation Dr., Bluffton, SC 29901
Replica hardware and accessories (many found nowhere else). 300 styles of door and cabinet hardware, weathervanes, tin ceilings, and cast iron barn bells, boot scrapers and horse hitches. Free Catalog. Phone: 800 422-9982, extension 1600. Fax: 803 837-9789. E-Mail: treasure@hargray.com. Website: antiquehardware.com.
Antique Hardware, New Hardware, Cupolas, Weathervanes

Antique Woods & Colonial Restoration

1273 Reading Ave., Boyertown, PA 19512
Restoration and reproduction of colonial structures, timber frame barns, outbuildings, log homes and stone structures. Their service area includes PA, NY, NJ, CT, DE, MD, VA. They dismantle, re-erect and convert antique frames, and provide resawn siding and flooring. Free literature. Phone: 610 367-8193. Fax: 610 367-6911. E-mail: antiquewds@aol.com.
Vintage Timber Frames and Log Homes, Restoration Services, Custom Design

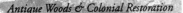

Antique Woods & Colonial Restoration

Architectural Antiques Exchange

715 North 2nd Street, Philadelphia, PA 19123
Architectural salvage including doors, street lamps, leaded and beveled glass, signs, paneling and much more. Free catalog. Phone: 215 922-3669. Fax: 215 922-3680.
Architectural Salvage

Architectural Iron Company - Capital Cresting

PO Box 126, Milford, PA 18337
America's leading producer of roof cresting offers a complete line of lightweight, easy to install, economical to ship, unbreakable steel roof cresting, matching finials and snow guards. Custom sizes are available. Free catalog. Phone: 800 442-IRON. Fax: 717 296-IRON.
Finials, Cresting, Snow Guards

Architectural Reclamation, Inc.

312 South River Street, Franklin, OH 45005
Small family construction firm specializing in historic restoration and rehabilitation and serving southwest Ohio. They are experienced in structural repairs, log and timber frame work, masonry, custom woodworking, sheet-metal roofing and box gutters, plastering and more. Free literature. Phone: 513 746-8964. Fax: 513 746-7694. E-mail: mayapple@siscom.net.
Restoration Services

Arizona-Pacific Group

PO Box 2806, Prescott, AZ 86302
Complete "lock-tight" exterior shell packages for cedar homes, cottages and cabins. Many plans are available. The kits are easy to build yourself and ideal for rural and wilderness locations. Technical support is included. Free catalog. Phone: 888 358-1113. Fax: 520 771-1229. E-mail: geow@goodnet.com. Website: www.goodnet.com/~geow/.
Cabin and Cottage Building Kits

Ashland Barns

Ashland Barns

990BH Butlercreek, Ashland, OR 97520
Blueprints are available for 94 barns, stables, garages with workshops, storage buildings, sheds and country homes - all designed for efficiency, beauty and economy of construction. Plans range in price from $12 to $50. Catalog: $5.00 (refunded with plan order). Phone: 541 488-1541.
Building Plans

The Barn People

PO Box 4, Morgan Hill, South Woodstock, VT 05071-0004
Offering a wide variety of antique Vermont barn frames which have been dismantled and restored and can be reassembled anywhere in the United States. The Barn People also offer custom-made, hand-hewn backyard office frames in kit form. Free literature. Phone: 802 457-3356. Fax: 802 457-3358. E-Mail: barnman@souer.net.
Vintage Timber Frames, Restoration Services, Custom Design, Building Kits

Barns by Gardner, Ltd.

3833 West County Road 8, Berthoud, CO 80513
Custom design and building of pole barns and stables in northern Colorado. From simple loafing sheds to elegant showplace stables, Steve Gardner and his crew will build to the highest standards of quality, with the best materials, and at reasonable prices. Free literature. Phone: 970 532-3595.
Custom Barn and Stable Design & Building, Building Plans

BarnPlans

BarnPlans
41-049 Ehukai Street, Waimanalo, HI 96795-1665
Simple, concise and easy-to-read blueprints designed with the owner/builder in mind. They have five sizes of Gambrel barn design: 16,' 20,' 24,' 28' and 32' widths with lengths designed to be modified to any required dimension. Phone or Fax: 808 259-7028. E-mail: dano@barnplans.com. Website: http://www.barnplans.com.
Building Plans for Homes, Garages, Shops and Barns

Belcher's
2505 West Hillview Drive, Dalton, GA 30721
Pre-Civil War log cabins, weathered barn siding, split rails, hand-hewn beams. They consult on restoration of old log cabins. Free literature. Phone: 706 259-3482.
Architectural Salvage, Restoration Services

Berry Hill Ltd.
75 Burwell Road, St.Thomas, ON, Canada N5P 3R5
Country living and hobby farm specialists, offering garden equipment, antique reproduction lighting, hobby farm equipment and much more. Catalog: $3.00. Phone: 800 688-3072. Fax: 519 631-8935. E-mail: kfox@berryhill.on.ca. Website: www.berryhill.on.ca.
Cupolas, Light fixtures, Windmills, Weather Vanes

Better Barns

Bessler Stairway Company
3807 Lamar Ave., Memphis, TN 38118
A Bessler one-piece sliding stairway is an excellent choice for loft and attic access. Free catalog. Phone: 901 360-1900. Fax: 901 795-1253. E-Mail: bessler@bessler.com Website: www.bessler.com.
Pull-down Stairs

Better Barns
126 Main Street South, Bethlehem, CT 06751
Better Barns has been constructing upscale yard buildings in Connecticut for over twenty years. They pay meticulous attention to the details and quality of each of the small barns that they build and offer plans and hardware to homeowners outside of their area. Free catalog. Phone: 203 266-7989. Fax: 203 266-5352. E-mail: bbarns@hotmail.com. Website: http://betterbarns.8m.com.
Construction of Small Barns and Sheds, Building Plans

Big Spring Preservation Group, Inc.
1004 West Summer Street, Greenville, TN 37743
Specialists at dismantling and restoring antique log cabins, barns, outbuildings, garden sheds and timber frame barns and houses. The buildings can be reassembled anywhere. They offer a full line of antique building materials. Free product literature. Phone: 423 787-9373. Fax: 423 787-9312.
Vintage Timber Frames, Restoration Services, Garden Structures, Antique Cabins & Outbuildings

Big Spring Preservation Group, Inc.

Board & Beam Co.

60 Wykeham Road, Washington, CT 06793

Barns and houses dismantled, rebuilt and restored. They sell salvaged materials including beams, planks, doors, hardware and architectural details. They also provide restoration and building shoring services. Free literature. Phone: 860 868-6789. Fax: 860 868-0721. E-mail: bbeams@ct1.nai.net.

Antique Timber Frames, Salvaged Lumber, Woodwork Details and Barn Doors, Antique Hardware, Restoration Services

Bouvet USA, Inc.

540 De Haro Street, San Francisco, CA 94107

Decorative hardware company, established in 1884, offers a wide selection of hand-forged iron hardware. The products are made in France and adapted to US standards. Free catalog. Phone: 415 864-0273. Fax: 800-ATBOUVET. E-Mail: info@bouvet.com.

Antique and Custom Hardware

Bow House/Bow Bends

PO Box 900, Bolton, MA 01740

Makers of fine quality traditional cottages and garages plus exotic garden structures: bridges, gazebos, arbors, follies, privies and trellises. Catalog: $5.00. Phone: 978 779-6464. Fax: 978 779-2272.

Garden Structures, Building Kits

Brandywine Valley Forge

P.O. Box 1129, Valley Forge, PA 19481-9998

Restoration blacksmiths specializing in hand-forged hardware, including strap hinges and pintles, hooks and hasps, barn door and gate bolts. They welcome custom work. Catalog; $5.00 or send a self-addressed stamped envelope for free literature. Phone: 610 948-5116. Fax: 610 933-4305.

Hand Forged Hardware

Brosamer's Bells

207 Irwin Street, Brooklyn, MI 49230

Bells for barn yards, backyards, cupolas, etc. Brass, cast iron and bronze, antique and new. Brosamer's is the country's largest dealer of pre-owned bells. Free product literature. Phone: 517 592-9030. Fax: 517 592-4511.

Barn and Yard Bells

Cannonball: HNP

555 Lawton Ave., Beloit, WI 53512

Cannonball: HNP is an 83 year old company that produces sliding door systems, tracks, trolleys, windows, walk doors, dutch doors, horse stalls, foil insulation, ventilators and cupolas for the agricultural marketplace. Free catalog. Phone: 800 766-2825. Fax: 608 365-4565. E-mail: cnbhnp@aol.com. Website: cnbhnp.com.

Doors, Windows, Hardware and Specialties for Barns, Stables and Agricultural Buildings

Cape Cod Cupola Co., Inc.

78 State Road, North Dartmouth, MA 02747

Cape Cod Cupola Company manufactures cupolas and weathervanes and specializes in custom work for both. They have a large selection of cupolas, weathervanes, sundials and house signs. Catalog: $2.00, refundable with first order. Phone: 508 994-2119. Fax: 508 997-2511.

Cupolas, Weathervanes

Chestnut Oak Co.

3810 Old Mountain Road, West Suffield, CT 06093-2125

Chestnut Oak Co. erects new timber frame structures throughout New England and New York. They also dismantle, move and erect old timber frame homes and barns. Product literature is free. Phone: 860 668-0382. Fax: 860 668-0382.

Antique Timber Frames, New Timber Frames, Historic Preservation Consultation

Christian & Son, Inc.

15022 Gearhart Road, Burbank, OH 44214

Specialists at designing, building and restoring barns, sheds and timber frame homes. Their new designs are based on the old ways of building and they work just as well today. Consultations are available. Phone: 330 624-7282. Fax: 330 624-0501. E-mail: rudad@aol.com.

Vintage Timber Frames, New Timber Frames, Restoration Services

CinderWhit & Company

733 Eleventh Avenue South, Wahpeton, ND 58075

Offers stock, replica or custom turnings, including porch posts, finials, newel posts, balusters and spindles for exterior and interior applications. Free brochure. Phone: 800 527-9064. Fax: 701 642-4204.

Wood Turnings

Colonial Barn Restoration

267 Old Bay Road, Bolton, MA 01740

Antique timber frame restoration and rebuilding, custom cupolas, cupola and steeple restoration and rebuilds, structural member replacement using mortise and tenon joinery. They serve the northeast USA. Phone or Fax: 978 779-9865. E-mail: tmurphy@aol.com.

Restoration Services, Cupolas

Colonial Cupolas, Inc.

1816 Nemoke Trail, P.O. Box 38, Haslett, MI 48840

America's largest selection of cupolas, assembled or as kits. Catalog: $3.00. Product Literature: $3.00. Phone: 517 349-6185.

Cupolas, Weathervanes, Sundials, Cast Metal Date and Street Number Plaques

Connolly & Co. Timber Frame Homes and Barns

10 Atlantic Highway, Edgecomb, ME 04556

Connolly & Co. restores existing timber frame structures; custom designs, cuts and erects homes, barns, outbuildings, additions, and truss systems; and offers four styles of pre-cut barn kits. Free literature. Phone: 207 882-4224. Fax: 207 882-4247. E-mail: connolly@lincoln.midcoast.com. Website: www.connollytimberframes.com.

Vintage Timber frames, New Timber Frames, Restoration Services, Barn Building Kits

Coppercraft, Inc.

2143 Joe Field Road, Suite 100, Dallas, TX 75229

Coppercraft utilizes traditional metalworking skills and modern technology to create high quality architectural sheet metal products including cupolas, spires, weathervanes and more. Free catalog and product literature. Phone: 800 486-2723. Fax: 972 484-3008. E-Mail: info@coppercraft.com Website: www.coppercraft.com.

Cupolas, Finals, Spires, Gutters, Vents, Roofing

The Copper House

1747 Dover Road (Route 4), Epsom, NH 03234-4416

Offers brass and copper interior and exterior lighting and copper weathervanes. All products are made in New Hampshire. Lighting is U.L. approved. Catalog: $4.00. Phone: 800 281-9798. Fax: 603 736-9798. Website: www.northwindnh.com/copper.

Post Lamps, Carriage House Lamps, Weathervanes

Country Carpenters, Inc.

326 Gilead Street (Route 85), Hebron, CT 06248

Designers and manufacturers of fine pre-cut, New England style post and beam barns, carriage houses, garages and sheds. Catalog: $4.00. Phone: 860 228-2276. Fax: 860 228-5106. Website: www.countrycarpenters.com.

Building Kits

Country Settings, Inc.

3305 West 4th Ave., Suite C, Belle WV 25015
Specialists in the recovery of authentic 150 year old hand-hewn log cabins and barns. They have a large inventory of antique log cabins and barns. Any of them can be reassembled on your site. Other vintage materials include resawn chestnut and oak, hand-cut stone, split-rail fence and weathered barnboard. Phone: 304 925-3863. Fax: 304 925-3303. E-mail: handhewn@aol.com. Website: www.countrysettings.com.
Vintage Hand Hewn Log Cabins, Antique Timber Frames and Building Materials, Restoration Services

Country Settings, Inc.

Craftwright Incorporated

100 Railroad Ave., Suite 105, Westminister, MD 21157
Custom, hand-crafted timber frames. Antique timbers and frames are available. Phone: 410 876-0999.
Vintage Timber Frames, New Timber Frames

Crosswinds Gallery, Inc.

29 Buttonwood Street, Bristol, RI 02809
Offers a large selection of quality weathervanes, cupolas and finials in a variety of materials and at a variety of prices. Crosswinds Gallery specializes in custom design and crafting. Imagine a weather vane, and they'll make it for you. Extensive catalog of designs is free. Phone: 401 253-0334. Fax: 401 253-2830. E-mail: wvanes@aol.com. Website: www.crosswinds.gallery.com.
Weathervanes, Finials, Cupolas, Custom Design

Cumberland General Store

#1 Highway 68, Crossville, TN 38555
General merchandise catalog with old-time and country specialties and restoration and building products. Weathervanes, boot scrapers, hitching posts, farm bells, farmstead tools, hardware, country home plans, pumps, windmills and building books. Catalog: $4.00. Phone: 931 484-8481. Fax: 931 456-1211. E-mail: generalstore@worldnet.att.net Website: www.cumberlandgeneral.com.
Hardware, Books, Building Plans, Weathervanes

Cumberland Woodcraft Company

P.O. Drawer 609, 10 Stover Drive, Carlisle, PA 17013
Provides interior and exterior Victorian millwork, gables, balustrades, corbels and brackets, mouldings and custom items. Catalog: $5.00. Phone: 800 367-1884. Fax: 717 243-6502. E-Mail: cwc@pa.net Website: www.pa.net/cwc/.
Woodwork, Finials & Cresting

Custom Home Plans, Inc.

Route 1, Lake Burton, Tiger, GA 30576
Offers over 100 country home plans that adapt to your lifestyle. Layouts are space-saving and have well thought out traffic patterns. Catalog, *Country Plans by Natalie*: $14.95. Phone or Fax: 706 782-5637. E-mail: nhoward@stc.net. Website: natalieplans.com.
Building Plans for Country Homes and Log Cabins, Custom Design

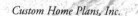

Custom Home Plans, Inc.

Dad's Woodshop

19392 Renwood Ave., Euclid, OH 44119
Dad's is a full service custom woodshop focusing on specialty and hard-to-find products. Product literature: $1.00. Phone: 216 383-8808.
Woodwork, Cupolas, Arbors, Trellises

Davis Frame Company

Dalton Pavilions, Inc.

20 Commerce Drive, Telford, PA 18969
Dalton Pavilions Inc. offers fine western red cedar prefabricated pavilions and garden structures that can be shipped throughout the U.S. and internationally. Free catalog. Phone: 215 721-1492. Fax: 215 721-1501.
Prefabricated Garden Structures

Davis Frame Company

PO Box 1079, Claremont, NH 03743
Specialists at designing and hand-crafting timber frames for homes and additions in new Douglas fir, pine, oak or reclaimed timbers with mortise and tenon joinery, chamfered edges and curved braces. Packages include the frame, stress skin panels, exterior finish materials, windows and doors. Free flyer. Catalog and Plan Portfolio: $15.00. Phone or Fax: 800 636-0993. E-mail: inquiry@davisframe.com. Website: www.davisframe.com.
New Timber Frame Home Building Kits, Custom Design

Denninger Weather Vanes & Finials

77 B Whipple Road, Middletown, NY 10940
Weather vanes featuring finely hand-crafted horses, roosters, eagles, banners, scrolls, arrows, caps and finials. They offer custom and standard designs, farm and business logos, and historic replications. They have an informative website for anyone interested in the art and lore of weather vanes. Free literature. Phone or Fax: 914 343-2229. E-Mail: al@denninger.com. Website: www.denninger.com.
Weather Vanes, Finials

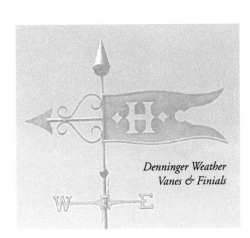

Denninger Weather Vanes & Finials

Dreaming Creek Timber Frame Homes, Inc.

2487 Judes Ferry Road, Powhatan, VA 23139
Custom timber framing and design of homes, churches, covered bridges, gazebos and barns. They erect frames, install structural panels, and supply timber, oak plank flooring and paneling. Free literature. Literature and video: $10.00. Phone: 804 598-4328. Fax: 804 598-3748. E-mail: dctfh@aol.com. Website: www.dreamingcreek.com.
New Timber Frames, Timber Frame Trusses, Custom Design, Garden Structures

Eagle Creek Designs, Inc.

6025 Schustrich Road, P.O. Box 163, Mantua, OH 44255
Eagle Creek Designs stocks log houses, timber frames, cut sandstone, ornamental stone, mantles, flooring, hardware, beadboard and beams. Phone 330 274-2041 for more information.
Building Materials, Vintage Timber Frames and Log Homes

Emerald Woodworking

21 Elbormar Drive, Huntington, NY 11743
Offers cedar ventilating louvers in any shape or size, exterior shutters, rough-hewn pine planking, board and batten doors and custom woodwork. Their service area is New York and New England. Free literature - send S.A.S.E. to the address above. Phone: 516 754-0377. Fax: 516 935-7546.
Woodwork

Eugenia's Antique Hardware

5370 Peachtree Road, Chamblee, GA 30341
Provides authentic antique hardware, including door and furniture hardware, hinges, handles, latches, knockers, mechanical bells and forged iron strap hinges. Catalog: $1.00. Phone: 800 337-1677. Fax: 770 458-5966.
Antique Hardware

Fingerlakes Weathervanes and Cupolas

P.O. Box 554, Canandaigua, NY 14424
Unique copper and brass weathervanes, made in the U.S.A. They create combination brass and copper American flag weather vanes. Free catalog and product literature. Phone: 716 394-1091.
Weather Vanes, Finials & Cresting

Garden Oak Specialties

1921 Route 22 West, Bound Brook, NJ 08805
Manufacturers of high quality, prefab garden buildings including sheds, gazebos, arbors, playhouses and mailboxes in a variety of styles. Buildings are shipped complete to your backyard. Free literature. Phone: 800 590-7433. Fax: 732 356-7202. E-mail: info@gardenoaks.com Website: www.gardenoaks.com.
Prefabricated Sheds and Garden Buildings

Gardensheds

651 Millcross Road, Lancaster, PA 17601
Classic designs of outbuildings and garden sheds. Complete buildings, hand-crafted of fine woods, are delivered to your property. Custom designs and building plans are also available. Portfolio: $5.00. Phone: 717 397-5430. Fax: 717 397-0217. Website: www.gardensheds.com.
Prefabricated Sheds and Garden Buildings, Custom Design, Building Plans

Gardensheds

Great Northern Barns

Box 912E, RFD 2, Canaan, NH 03741
Great Northern Barns works with all aspects of timber framing with an emphasis on providing and erecting antique barn frames. Free literature. Video: $10.00. Phone: 603 523-7134. Fax: 603 523-7134. Website: www.greatnorthernbarns.com.
Vintage Timber Frames

Gothic Arch Greenhouses

P.O. Box 1564-BB, Mobile, AL 36633
Gothic Arch Greenhouses, a division of Trans-Sphere Trading Corp., creates beautiful Gothic style greenhouse kits in redwood, with polycarbonate glazing, in sizes for hobby, backyard or commercial use. Designs are freestanding or lean-to. They also provide heating, cooling, ventilation and humidification systems for greenhouses. Product literature: $2.00. Phone: 334 432-7529. Fax: 334 432-7972.
Greenhouse Kits and Environmental Systems

Green Star Forge

3 Myrtle Street, Taunton, MA 02780-4111
One-man shop specializing in custom forged iron work. Catalog: $2.00. Phone: 508 824-3077.
Hand Forged Iron Hardware

Habitat Post & Beam

Habitat Post & Beam

21 Elm Street, South Deerfield, MA 01373
Habitat Post & Beam pre-manufacturers material packages for post and beam homes and additions. Their in-house design and engineering services allow you to custom design your project to fit your personal vision. They can work from your ideas, your architect's design or a plan from an extensive library of designs. Catalog: $12.00 (it's downloadable at their website). Phone: 800 992-0121. Fax: 413 665-4008. E-mail: sales@postandbeam.com. Website: www.postandbeam.com.
Home Building Kits, Manufactured Buildings, New Timber Frames, Custom Design

Hager Companies

139 Victor Street, St.Louis, MO 63104
Manufacturer of hinges and builders' hardware including barn door rollers, tracks and accessories, strap hinges, shed hardware, metal thresholds, door sweeps and gate hardware. Free catalog and product literature. Phone: 314 772-4400. Fax: 314 772-0744.
Hardware, Barn Door Rollers & Track

Hahn Woodworking Company, Inc.

109 Aldene Road, Roselle, NJ 07203
Custom wooden garage doors built to your specifications. They offer stile and rail doors with flat or raised panels, historic barn and carriage-house style doors with convenient overhead motorized operation, traditional swing-out doors and sliding doors. Free catalog and product literature. Phone: 908 241-8825. Fax: 908 241-9293.
Barn & Garage Doors, Custom Design

Handy Home Products

Handy Home Products

6400 E.11 Mile Road, Warren, MI 48091
North America's largest manufacturer of ready-to-assemble wooden storage buildings, gazebos, timber buildings, solar sheds and playhouses. Their buildings are sold through home centers. Free catalog. Phone: 800 221-1849. Fax: 810 757-6066. Website: www.handyhome.com.
Building Kits for Cabins, Garages, Storage Sheds, Solar Sheds, Gazebos and Playhouses

William T. Hardy, Builder

Rural Route 2, Box 344, North Bennington VT 05257
Custom builder of country homes and barns. Hardy provides fine craftsmanship in pole-framing, light-frame and log construction in southern Vermont, northwestern Massachusetts and eastern New York. Phone: 802 442-4075
Custom Builder

Healthy Home Designs

PO Box 41124, Des Moines, IA 50311
Provides blueprints, eco specs and consultation services. They are dedicated to designing eco-centered dwellings that positively promote the wellness of their occupants while using sustainable building materials. Catalog: $28.00. Free brochure. Phone: 515 255-1425. Fax: 515 255-6145. E-mail: healthyhom@aol.com. Website: www.energybuilder.com/healthyhomedesigns.
Building Plans, Publications

Historic Housefitters Co.

P.O. Box 26, 32 Centre, Route 312, Brewster, NY 10509
Offers hand-forged iron hardware of all types, including strap hinges and pintles, cane bolts, thumb latches, door pulls. Stock hardware, custom designs and reproductions. Catalog: $3.00. Phone: 914 278-2427. Fax: 914 278-7726.
New Hardware, Custom Reproductions

Holmes Garage Door

P.O. Box 1976, Auburn, WA 98071-1976
Holmes Garage Door manufactures a complete line of custom, hand-crafted wood garage doors. The "Carriage House" door is a wood roll-down that simulates historic swinging doors. Free product literature. Phone: 253 931-8900. Fax: 253-939-8508.
Barn & Garage Doors

Honest Abe Log Homes, Inc.

3855 Clay County Highway, Moss, TN 38575
Manufacturers of log home and timber frame pre-cut kits, using your plans
or one of their own standard plans. They offer complete design services,
delivery anywhere and building crews to construct the kits to a dried-in
stage. Free literature. Catalog: $10.00. Video: $10.00. CD: $10.00. All
three: $25.00. Phone: 800 231-3695. Fax: 931 258-3397. E-mail:
honestabe@multipro.com. Website: www.honestabe.com.
Log and Timber Frame Home Building Kits, Custom Design

Honest Abe Log Homes, Inc.

Ken Hume, Engineer

Oakhurst, Sherfield Road, Bramley, Hampshire, England RG26 5AQ
Registered professional engineer practicing in the USA and UK. Timber-
frame designer and structural analyst with an understanding of traditional
practices in America and Europe. Phone: 011 44 1256 881344. E-mail:
ken.hume@pareuro.com.
Timber Frame Engineering, Restoration Services

Independent Protection Co., Inc.

1603-09 South Main Street, P.O. Box 537, Goshen, IN 46527
Ornamental and conventional lightning protection equipment, systems and
products for all types of homes, barns and related structures. Catalog:
$10.00. Product literature: $5.00. Phone: 219 533-4116. Fax: 219 534-
3719. E-Mail: ipc@netbahn.net.
Lightning Rods, Weather Vanes

Iron Intentions Forge

RD#2, Box 2399C, Spring Grove, PA 17362
Custom forged hardware and accents in steel, stainless, brass, copper and
aluminum. Phone: 717 229-2665.
Antique Hardware, New Hardware, Weather Vanes

Ives Weathervanes

Box 101A, RR1, Charlemont, MA 01339
Hand-formed, elegant custom copper and brass weather vanes. Ives
Weathervanes creates three-dimensional hammer formed vanes with
"chased" in details and two-dimensional silhouette style pieces. Gold leafing
is available. Catalog: $1.00. Phone: 413 339-8534.
Weather Vanes

Jack's Country Store

P.O. Box 710, Bay Avenue & Highway 103, Ocean Park, WA 98640
Jack's genuine Alladin kerosene lamps are smokeless, odorless and as bright
as a 60-watt light bulb. The lamps are great for nonelectric buildings. Jack's
offers a complete selection of lamps and parts. Catalog: $1.00. Phone: 360
665-4988. Fax: 360 665-4989.
Kerosene Lamps, Hardware

Kayne & Son Custom Hardware, Inc.

100 Daniel Ridge Road, Chandler, NC 28715
Custom forged hardware, strap hinges, latches, bolts, braces, door rollers,
hasps, locks, branding irons, restoration, repairs and reproduction of
antique hardware. Catalog: $5.00. Phone: 704 667-8868. Fax: 704 665-
8303. E-Mail: kaynehdwe@ioa.com.
New Forged Hardware, Restoration Services

Landmark Services, Inc.
7 Oakland Street, Medway, MA 02053
Landmark Services, Inc. is a restoration and renovation general contracting firm specializing in the restoration of historic homes, barns and churches.sembled and reassembled. Free literature. Phone or Fax: 508 533-8393. E-Mail: landmark@gis.net. Website: www.landmarkservices.com
Restoration Services

Lehman's
One Lehman Circle, P.O. Box 41, Kidron, OH 44636
Lehman's 160 page nonelectric catalog contains 2,500 items you thought weren't made any more, including farm tools, wood stoves, grain mills, butter churns, copper kettles and more. Catalog: $3.00. Phone: 330 857-5757. Fax: 330 857-5785. E-Mail: info@lehmans.com.
Hardware, How-to Books, Tools, Gas Lamps

Lemee's Fireplace Equipment
815 Bedford Street, Bridgewater, MA 02324
Provides wrought-iron hardware, strap hinges, boot scrapers, barn bells and gongs, hitching posts and weather vanes. Catalog: $2.00. Phone: 508 697-2672.
Antique Hardware, New Hardware, Weather Vanes

Lester Building Systems
1111 2nd Avenue South, Lester Prairie, MN 55354
Lester Building Systems, a division of Butler Manufacturing Company, manufactures pre-engineered wood-frame structures for agricultural, equestrian, commercial and suburban use. Product literature is available. Phone: 800 826-4439. Fax: 320 395-2969. E-Mail: marketing@lesterbuildingsystems.com. Website: www.lesterbuildingsystems.com.
Pre-engineered Post-Frame Buildings, Custom Design

The Mailbox Shoppe
2566A Hempstead Turnpike, East Meadow, NY 11554
The Mailbox Shoppe represents over 30 manufacturers of weathervanes, cupolas, mailboxes, mailbox posts, custom cast signs and other home accessories. Free catalog and product literature. Phone: 800 330-3309. Fax: 516 735-6191. E-mail: sales@mailboxnet.com Website: www.mailboxnet.com.
Mailboxes, Cupolas, Weather Vanes

The Mailbox Source
12367 Deerbrook Lane, Los Angeles, CA 90049-1909
Residential freestanding and wall-mounted mailboxes in a wide variety of styles and materials. They offer locking boxes, large capacity boxes and novelty boxes. Free catalog. Phone or Fax: 800 209-0111.
Mailboxes

Sam Marts Architects and Planners/ White Oak Timber Frame
2104 West Wabansia, Chicago, IL 60647
Professional architects and builders provide integrated design and timber frame construction services for clients, worldwide. Phone: 773 862-0123. Fax: 773 862-0173. E-mail: info@timbersmart.com. Website: www.timbersmart.com.
Custom Design, New Timber Frames

Meyers Restoration & Architectural Salvage
R2 Box 1250, East River Road, Clinton, ME 04927
Restoration, preservation and reproduction of 18th and 19th century buildings. They provide carpentry services from frame repair to reproduction millwork, period consulting and planning. They also buy and sell antique architectural details and building materials. Free literature. Phone: 207 453-7010. Fax: 207 238-9905. E-mail: myrest@mint.net.
Architectural Antiques, Antique Timber Frames, Woodwork, Restoration Services

John T. Miller, Barnbuilders

229 Church Street, East Harwich, MA 02645
New England style barns, garages, sheds, pool houses, small bridges and related breezeways and connectors built on Cape Cod, South East Massachusetts and New Hampshire. Miller Barnbuilders work in modified timber frame construction. They try to incorporate interesting salvaged millwork and hardware into their projects to give each a one-of-a-kind look. Project photos available on request. Phone: 508 430-0684.
Custom Barn Builders, Restoration Services

John T. Miller, Barnbuilders

The Millworks, Inc.

P.O. Box 2987, Durango, CO 81302
Offers Victorian, traditional, country and southwest millwork. Catalog: $2.00. Phone: 970 259-5915. Fax: 970 259-5919.
Woodwork

Mink Hill Timber Frame Homes, Inc.

285 Davis Road, Bradford, NH 03221
Builder of timber frame homes and barns. Mink Hill provides architectural design and engineering services, supply antique barns and restore existing barns. Free literature. Phone or Fax: 603 938-5203. E-mail: kwhitehead@conknet.com.
New Timber Frames, Vintage Timber Frames, Custom Design, Restoration Services

Mink Hill Timber Frame Homes, Inc.

Mountain Construction Enterprises

PO Box 1177, Boone, NC 28607
Builds timber frame, log, and other custom buildings. They will ship building kits nationwide or build complete homes in North Carolina. Free literature. Catalog: $12.00. Phone: 828 264-1231. Fax: 828 264-4863. E-mail: mtnconst@boone.net. Website: www.mountainconstruction.com.
Log and Timber Frame Home Building Kits, Custom Design

New Energy Works Timberframers

1755 Pioneer Road, Shortsville, NY 14548
New Energy Works Timberframers designs and builds timber frame homes and structures of the highest quality. Their projects represent a philosophy of individual attention to the client and to the building process. Free literature. Phone: 716 298-3220. E-mail: jonathan@newenergyworks.com. Website: www.newenergyworks.com.
New Timber Frames, Custom Design, Vintage Timber Frames.

New England Barn Company

New England Barn Company

63 Gaylord Road, Gaylordsville, CT 06755
Creates precut timber frame barns fashioned in the classic New England style, with authentic mortise and tenon joinery. A variety of sizes and styles are available, and custom work is welcomed. Free literature. Phone or Fax: 860 350-5544.
Barn Kits, New Timber Frames

New England Cupola

184 Mattapoisett Road, Acushnet, MA 02743
Builder of fine, hand-crafted cupolas in a wide range of styles and sizes. Custom work is New England Cupola's specialty. Free catalog and product literature. Phone: 508 995-5331. Fax: 508 998-7041.
Cupolas, Weather Vanes, Custom Design

New England Outbuildings

P.O. Box 621, Westbrook, CT 06498
New England Outbuildings creates new farm and garden outbuildings in the traditional manner by meticulously preserving the lines, proportion and details of New England's historic buildings. Post and beam frames are milled from oak, cut with mortise and tenon joints and shipped to your site to be assembled with wooden pegs. Frame kits include designs for barns, wagon sheds, corn cribs and more. Free literature. Phone: 860 669-1776.
New Timber Frames, Building Kits

New Jersey Barn Company

PO Box 702, Princeton, NJ 08542
New Jersey Barn Company offers antique oak barn timber frames which they re-erect on your property. Free literature. Phone: 609 924-8480. Fax 609 730-1030.
Vintage Timber Frames

Niagara Designs, Inc.

PO Box 191, Niagara Falls, ON, Canada L2E 6T3
Provides stock construction plans for garden structures, including gazebos, sheds, playhouses, greenhouses, garages and more. Plans can be used for do-it-yourself projects or by your builder. E-mail: plans@niagaradesigns.com. Website: www.niagaradesigns.com.
Building Plans

Niagara Designs, Inc.

Northeastern Log Homes, Inc.

PO Box 46, Kenduskeag, ME 04450
Manufacturers of premium log home packages as well as vacation and small getaway camps and cabins. Plan book and catalog: $10.00. Phone: 800 624-2797. Website: www.northeasternlog.com.
Log Home Building Kits

North Woods Joinery

PO Box 1166, Burlington, VT 05402-1166
Creates traditional post and beam structures, including gazebos, barns, sheds and homes. Your choice of wood species includes pine, hemlock, oak and Douglas fir. Free product literature. Phone: 802 644-2400 or 802 644-2500. Fax: 802 644-2509.
New Timber Frames, Building Kits

O'Brock Windmills

9435 12th Street, North Benton, OH 44449
O'Brock Windmills sells and installs old style water pumping windmills which are very often found next to old country homes and barns. They were, and still are, used to provide water for livestock. Today, many people install them just to look good turning in the breeze. Catalog: $2.00. Phone: 330 584-4681. Fax: 330 584-4682. E-Mail: windmill@cannet.com.
Water Pumping Windmills, Hand Pumps, Hydraulic Rams

David D. Parker, Structural Restoration

904 Upper Dummerston Road, Brattleboro, VT 05301
Provides restoration consulting and contract services, 18th and 19th century timber frames and antique lumber. Phone: 802 257-5717. Fax: 802 257-5719. E-mail: sjmpr@sover.net. Website: parkerrestoration.com.
Restoration Services, Vintage Timber Frames, Antique Building Materials

David D. Parker, Structural Restoration

Rapid River Rustic, Inc.

PO Box 10, Rapid River, MI 49878
Rapid River Rustic manufactures cedar log homes. They specialize in custom design and can provide a full set of blueprints and material to build your cedar log home. Free literature. Catalog: $10.00. Phone: 800 422-3327. Fax: 906 474-6500. E-mail: rrrustic@up.net. Website: www.rapidriverrustic.com.
Log Home Building Kits, Custom Design

Real Log Homes

PO Box 202, Hartland, VT 05048
Real Log Homes offers numerous distinct styles of log profiles from three plants across the U.S. For over 35 years they've offered precision pre-cut home kits, countless options, and innovative design, technology and manufacturing. Free literature. Plan Book: $10.00. Phone: 800 732-5564. Fax: 802 436-2150. Website: www.realloghomes.com.
Pre-cut Log Homes

Selectimber Structures

Renovator's Supply

PO Box 2515, Conway, NH 03818-2515
Looking for something special? Renovator's Supply sells hard-to-find items for building and restoration projects. Products include wrought iron hardware, cupolas, weather vanes, mail boxes, garden furniture, light fixtures, reproduction materials, hardware and plumbing fixtures. Free catalog. Phone: 800 659-2211.
Reproduction Hardware and Building Products

Restoration Resources

Sheldon Designs/MicroLodge

167 Dock Road, Alna, ME 04535
Specializes in period restoration of 18th century buildings in the state of Maine. Professional services include consultation, house inspection, fine carpentry, and restoration or relocation of early structures. Free literature. Phone: 207 586-5680. E-mail: fossel@oldhouserestoration.com. Website: www.oldhouserestoration.com.
Restoration Services, Vintage Timber Frames, Antique Hardware and Building Components

Recycled Products Company

18294 Amber Road X44, Monticello, IA 52310-7708
Manufacturer of plastic lumber and "100 Year" windows, recycled from milk containers. White, venting barn windows are USDA approved, never need paint or putty, come in a variety of efficient, attractive sizes and help reduce landfill waste. Free product literature. Phone: 800 765-1489. Fax: 319 465-1489.
Barn Sash and Windows, Recycled Lumber

RiverSong Art & Design

RiverSong Art & Design

R.R.#4, Quyon, Quebec, Canada J0X 2V0
Since 1984, RiverSong has been creating custom designs of hand-crafted log homes and cottages that grow out of the dreams of their owners and the spirit of the land. They serve eastern Canada and the northeast USA. Free literature. Phone or Fax: 819 647-6365. E-mail: rivsong@indelta.com. Website: http://riversong.indelta.com.
Custom Log Home Design, Building Plans

Royalston Oak Timber Frame

122 North Fitzwilliam Road, Royalston, MA 01331
New England and medieval English timber frames in oak, pine, hemlock and fir. The artisans of Royalston Oak work with the highest quality timbers and provide traditional joinery. Catalog: $8.00. Free literature. Phone: 800 317-1129. Fax: 978 249-9633.
New Timber Frames, Medieval English-Style Timber Frames

Salter Industries

P.O. Box 183, Eagleville, PA 19408
Manufacturer of steel and wood spiral stairs in a variety of sizes and designs including half-turns and units that meet BOCA and UBC code requirements. Free literature. Phone: 610 631-1306. Fax: 610 631-9384.
Spiral Stairs

Second Harvest Salvage

RR#1, Box 194-E, Jeffersonville, VT 05464
Provides antique hand-hewn barn and house frames, wide board flooring, beams and other antique building materials. Second Harvest also provides consultation on building restoration. Call for information. Phone: 802 644-8169.
Vintage Timber Frames, Restoration Services

Sentry Handcrafted Log Homes

PO Box 969, Grand Marais, MN 55604
A family run hand-crafted log home construction business, serving Minnesota, Wisconsin and adjacent states. Products and services include log construction, construction planning, log timber framing, and log architectural components. Free literature. Planning Guide: $7.50. Phone: 218 387-2644. Fax: 218 387-2740. E-mail: logs@sentry.com. Website: www.sentry.com.
Custom Log Homes

Selectimber Structures

River Street Factory, PO Box 293, Windsor, VT 05098
Timber frame and stress-skin panel home manufacturer specializing in engineered wood timbers with patented Timberlok mortise and tenon joinery. Unique "Acadia 3014" kit cottage can be shipped worldwide. Free brochure on the Lighthouse Kit Cottage. A package with Acadia 3014 design drawings, specifications and Timberlok video is available for $35.00. Phone: 802 674-6145. Fax: 802 674-6659. E-Mail: jack@ttlc.net. Website: www.selectimber.com.
Building Kits, New Timber Frames, Custom Design

Sheldon Designs/MicroLodge

1330 Route 206, #204, Skillman, NJ 08558
MicroLodge is a genuine log cabin kit that comes in a complete, easy-to-assemble package that can be placed virtually anywhere. Use it as a hunting cabin, retreat, pool house, guest house, etc. Free literature. Video: $9.95. Phone: 800 572-5934. Fax: 609 683-5976. E-mail: andysheldon@worldnet.att.net. Website: sheldondesigns.com.
Log Cabin Building Kits

Shelter-Kit Incorporated

22 Mill Street, Tilton, NH 03276
Pre-cut post and beam houses, cabins and multi-purpose barns are sold in kit form. These buildings are designed specifically for owner assembly. No construction skills or power tools are needed. Free literature. Phone: 603 286-7611. Fax: 603 286-2839. E-mail: buildings@shelter-kit.com. Website: www.shelter-kit.com.
Country Home, Cabin and Barn Building Kits

Singletree & Associates

19840 Rocking Horse Road, Bend, OR 97702
Restoration and repair of log, timber frame and conventionally framed structures. Services are provided from assessments through "hands-on" construction. Singletree & Associates also builds new barns and outbuildings. Phone: 541 382-7143.
Log and Timber Frame Building, Restoration Services

Spiral Stairs of America, Inc.

1700 Spiral Court, Erie, PA 16510-1367
Manufacturer of spiral, curved and straight stair systems for indoor and outdoor use. Stairs are made of steel, wood or aluminum. Free product literature. Phone: 800 422-3700. Fax: 814-899-9139.
Stairs

Southern Cypress Log Homes

20495 Beals Chapel Road, Lenoir City, TN 37772 and US Hwy. 19
South,Crystal River, FL 34423
Manufacturer of low-maintenance log homes of cypress, western red cedar and
redwood. These woods have a natural resistance to termites and decay. Catalog
and plan book: $4.95. Construction manual: $4.95. Phone: 352 705-0777.
Log Home Building Kits and Custom Design

Tamarack Log Building Tools, Inc.

PO Box 120783, New Brighton, MN 55112
Offers log building and logging tools and supplies. Tamarack's free catalog
includes an extensive list of building and country living books. Phone: 612
783-9773. E-mail: tamlogtool@aol.com.
Log Home Building Supplies and Guide Books

Texas Timber Frames

7214 Echert, San Antonio, TX 78238
Texas Timber Frames designs, engineers, joins and raises traditional old-world
handcrafted timber frame structures, timber trusses, timber roof systems and
architectural timber work. They also engineer and install structural insulated
paneling systems. Free literature. Phone: 210 647-4662. Fax: 210 647-4667.
E-mail: info@texastimberframes.com. Website: www.texastimberframes.com.
New Timber Frames, Custom Design

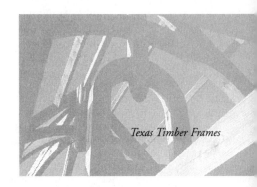

Texas Timber Frames

Timber & Stone Restorations

5431 East U.S. Highway 290, Fredericksburg, TX 78624
Timber & Stone salvages, restores and resells vintage log structures and timber
frames - from small smoke houses to 3,000+sf log barns. They also provide
antique material and accessories. Free literature. Video: $10.00. Phone: 830
997-2280. Fax: 830 997-1195. E-mail: magnum@ktc.com. Website:
timberandstone.com.
**Vintage Log Cabins, Log Barns, and Timber Frames, Antique Building
Materials, Restoration Services**

*Timber & Stone
Restorations*

Timber Creek Post and Beam Inc.

P.O. Box 309, Cuttingsville, VT 05738
Provides timber frame homes and barns, hand-crafted from eastern white pine
using traditional mortise and tenon joinery. Custom design, quality and
flexibility are part of Timber Creek's tradition. Free literature. Phone: 802 775-
6591. Fax: 802 775-6591. E-mail: timber@sover.net.
New Timber Frames, Custom Design

Timber Frames by R.A. Krouse

46 Titcomb Lane, Arundel, ME 04046
Complete traditionally joined barns, homes and other structures, delivered and
raised throughout New England. Frames are cut from white pine, selected from
Maine's western mountains. Resawn Douglass fir and white oak frames are also
available. Call for a house and barn tour. Free literature. Phone or Fax: 207
967-2747. E-mail: rakrouse@cybertours.com. Website:
www.mainetimberframes.com.
New Timber Frames, Custom Design, Timber Frame Garden Structures

Timber Creek Post and Beam Inc.

Timberpeg

PO Box 5474, West Lebanon, NH 03784
Hand-crafted, custom designed timber frame homes are offered in Douglas fir
or pine. Pre-cut packages are fabricated and shipped from east or west coast
facilities. Standard designs are also available. Catalog: $15.00. Free literature.
Phone: 603 542-7762. Fax: 603 542-8925. E-mail: info@timberpeg.com.
Website: www.timberpeg.com.
New Timber Frames, Custom Design

Vermont Stresskin Panels

184 John Putnam Memorial, Cambridge, VT 05444
Provides stresskin panel enclosure systems for timber frame structures. They provide fast, tight and economical shells for energy efficient homes. Free literature. Phone: 802 644-8885. Fax: 802 644-8797. E-mail: info@stresskin.com. Website: www.stresskin.com.
Stresskin Panels for Timber Frame Homes

Vermont Timber Frames

7 Pearl Street, Cambridge, NY 12816
Provides traditional timber frame structures for homes, barns, stables and outbuildings. Free literature. Phone: 518 677-8860. Fax: 518 677-3626. E-mail: tomharrison@vtf.com. Website: www.vtf.com.
New Timber Frames, Custom Design

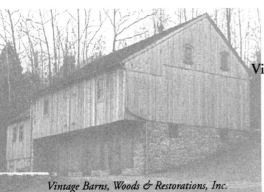

Vintage Barns, Woods & Restorations, Inc.

Vintage Barns, Woods & Restorations, Inc.

333 Mossy Brooks Road, High Falls, NY 12440
Specializes in the restoration and reproduction of colonial structures, timber frame barns, outbuildings, log homes and stone structures. Their primary area of service is the middle Atlantic states. They dismantle, re-erect and convert antique frames, and provide resawn siding and flooring. Free literature. Phone or Fax: 914 256-9564. E-mail: barns@hvi.net. Website: www.vintagewoods.com.
Vintage Timber Frames and Log Homes, Restoration Services, Custom Design

The Weather Hill Company

PO Box 113, Charlotte, VT 05445
Specialists in classic, traditional home design, restoration, reproduction woodwork and consultation. They work in New England and nationwide. The Westher Hill Company maintains an inventory of historic buildings which may be moved to your property. Free literature. Phone: 802 425-2095. Fax: 802 425-6402.
Restoration Services, Custom Design, Woodwork

Weather or Knot Antiques

8504 West 1350 S, P.O. Box 321, Wanatah, IN 46390
Provides antique and modern lightning rod glass ornaments, antique rods and weather vanes. They offer restoration material for lightning protection memorabilia. Catalog: $10.00. Phone: 219 733-2530.
Lightning Rods, Decorative Glass Insulators, Weather Vanes

West Coast Weather Vanes

377 Westdale Drive, Santa Cruz, CA 95060
West Coast Weather Vanes creates hand-crafted, limited-edition copper and brass weather vanes for residential, commercial and public facilities and gardens. 250 designs are available. Custom and personalized vanes can be commissioned. Free product literature. Phone: 800 762-8736. Fax: 408 425-5505. E-Mail: wcwvanes@ix.netcom.com.
Weather Vanes

Vermont Timber Frames

Wind & Weather

PO Box 2320, Mendocino, CA 95460
Wind & Weather's catalog offers weather vanes, cupolas and finials for all types of country homes, barns and outbuildings. Products include weather instruments, yard bells and chimes, wind sculptures, sundials and garden ornaments. Free catalog. Phone: 707 964-1284. Fax: 707 964-1278.
Cupolas, Weather Vanes, Garden Accessories

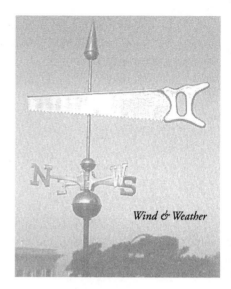

Wind & Weather

Windy Hill Forge

3824 Schroeder Ave., Perry Hall, MD 21128
Custom barn door strap hinges, large gate hinges, door hinges, bolts, hasps, cast iron wall washers; restoration work on antique iron hardware. Phone 410 256-5890. E-Mail: windyhillforge@juno.com.
New and Antique Forged Hardware

Woodcraft

P.O. Box 1686, Parkersburg, WV 26102
Woodcraft offers the highest quality woodworking tools including socket slicks, corner chisels, heavy duty framing chisels and adzes. Free catalog. Phone: 800 225-1153. Fax: 304 428-8271. Website: www.woodcraft.com
Woodworking Tools and Books

Woodhouse - The Timber Frame Company

Box 219, Route 549, Mansfield, PA 16933
and PO Box 1778, Breckenridge, CO 80424
Woodhouse is a custom manufacturer of timber frame house and barn kits. They use premium materials and craftsmanship. Their services range from architectural design through the construction of their packages. Catalog: $17.00. Phone: 800 227-4311. Fax: 570 549-6233. Website: www.woodhouse-pb.com.
New Timber Frame Home and Barn Kits, Custom Design

Wood House

PO Box 245, Ashton, ID 83420
Supplies all specialized tools and materials for log construction and provides the homeowner and the professional builder with the largest selection of quality products available. Catalog: $2.50. Phone 208 652-3608.
Log Home Building Tools

Wood's Metal Studios

6945 Fishburg Road, Huber Heights, OH 45424
Offers custom forging of traditional and contemporary ironwork, including gates, railings, stair rails, hardware, lighting, etc. Wood's Metal Studios can match your antique hardware. Phone: 937 233-6751.
Reproduction Hardware, Gates & Railings

Woodstock Log Home Services

10 Chenango Street, Cazenovia, NY 13035
Log home maintenance products and services - sealants, stains, chinking and caulking, leveling, rot repair; provides maintenance inspections and service contracts from coast to coast, through offices in Colorado, New York and North Carolina. Free literature. Phone: 888 483-5524. E-mail: woodstocklog@earthlink.net. Website: woodstocklog.com.
Log Home Restoration and Maintenance Services

George Yonnone, Restorations

PO Box 278, West Stockbridge, MA 01266
Specialist in timber frame structural repair, jacking, squaring and sill replacement. Yonnone can provide complete interior and exterior restoration, including dismantling and relocating antique structures and log cabins. Free literature. Phone: 413 232-7060.
Vintage Timber Frames and Log Cabins, Restoration Services

References & Resources

Building Codes

Your region is probably covered by one of the four major building codes. Call or write to get information or to order code books.

Building Officals & Code Administrators International (BOCA)
4051 West Flossmore Road, Country Club Hills, IL 60477
708 799-2300

International Code Council (ICC)
5203 Leesburg Pike, Falls Church, VA 22041
703 931-4533

International Conference of Building Officials (ICBO)
5360 South Workman Mill Road, Whittier, CA 90601
562 699-0541

Southern Building Code Congress International (SBCCI)
900 Montclair Road, Birmingham, AL 35213
205 591-1853

Building Book Catalogs

These organizations offer free catalogs full of hard-to-find books on building and woodworking specialties. Call or write them for your copy or visit their websites.

Builder's Booksource
1817 4th Street, Berkeley, CA 94710
Free Catalog. Phone: 510 845-6874.

Linden Publishing
336 West Bedford, #107, Fresno, CA 93711
Free *Woodworkers Library* catalog has over 300 books and videos.
Phone: 800 345-4447. Fax: 559 431-2327. Website: www.lindenpub.com

Home Builders Bookstore of the National Association of Home Builders
1201 15th Street, NW, Washington, DC 20005-2800
Free catalog offers guide books to help you work well with your home builder or remodeler. Resources on caring for your home and a wide variety of professionsl reference and "how-to" books for home builders.
Phone: 800 368-5242. Website: builderbooks.com.

Summer Beam Books
2299 Route 488, Clifton Springs, NY 14432
Free catalog of books on timber framing, woodworking, barns, house design and construction, and related crafts.
Phone: 877 279-1987, toll free. Fax: 716 289-3221. E-mail: char@fltg.net. Website: www.summerbeambooks.com.

On-Line Resources

BackHome Magazine has a variety of useful information on their website - great books on country building, homesteading and living with nature, articles from the latest issues of the magazine, and an on-line catalog of products and tools. You'll also find an index of back issues, with dozens of articles on traditional and unusual country building techniques. The website is: www.backhomemagazine.com.

B4UBUILD.COM is an on-line source of information about residential construction and design, the custom home building process, pictures of houses, pet peeves, book reviews, software, and a directory of homebuilding resources. You'll find the website at: http://www.b4ubuild.com.

The Barn Journal On-line is a website dedicated to the appreciation and preservation of traditional farm architecture. Editor Charles Leik reviews new publications and posts news about events and resources. The free classified ads are a terrific way to find restoration specialists, old barn frames and authentic hardware and fittings. Check it out at: http://museum.cl.msu.edu/barn.

Barn Again! is a website run by *Successful Farming Magazine* and The National Trust for Historic Preservation. It provides information to help owners of historic barns rehabilitate them and put them back to productive use. The website address is: htpp://www.agriculture.com/contents/ba!/ba!.html.

Farmer's Market Online will give you a taste of country life before you move. It's a great source for farm supplies, books, green house kits, seeds, recipes, herbs, sauces and spices. Log on at: wwwfarmersmarketonline.com.

The National Frame Builders Association posts a state by state directory of their members - professional "pole-barn" and home builders, designers, and manufacturers of country building materials. Visit the website: www.postframe.org, to find the pros in your area.

Timber Framing Magazine, has information on timber framing and alternative building. The website is: www.timberframingmagazine.com.

Illustration of the Brookfield House (see page 26), by Michigan artist Harry Wilson. Visit his website: www.pen-n-ink.com.

Country Building Guide Books

Backroad Homes

Build a Classic Timber-Framed House, by Jack Sobon. (Story Books, 1994) The plans, photos, patterns and details in this book can be used as a step-by-step guide to building a New England hall-and-parlor house. It's also a designer's guide, a history book and a great introduction to timber framing.

Build Your Own Low-Cost Log Home, by Roger Hard. (Story Books, 1985) This update of the classic 1977 book will help you choose a site, plan your cabin, find a kit or build from scratch. Easy to read text, illustrations, plans and details of a pretty 24' x 40', hillside cabin can be a do-it-yourself guide or can serve as inspiration for other cabin designs.

Complete Guide to Building Log Homes, by Monte Burch, Richard J. Meyer and Lloyd P. Birmingham. (Sterling Publications, 1990)
This how-to guide covers the log home building process from land planning through the time you enjoy the warmth of your new fireplace.

The Complete Guide to Log and Cedar Homes: All About Buying, Building, Decorating and Furnishing Log, Cedar and Post & Beam Homes, by Gary D. Branson. (Betterway Books, 1993) The best overall guide to understanding and working with log and timber frame manufacturers and building with their kits. This book includes a very complete directory of manufacturers, sources of building and maintenance supplies and 28 home plans.

Log Homes Made Easy: Contracting and Building Your Own Log Home, by Jim Cooper. (Stackpole Books, 1993) A how-to for the modern log home builder, this book focuses on comparing different manufacturers' kits and the process of planning, permits, financing and working with a log home contractor.

The Natural House Catalog: Everything You Need to Create an Environmentally Friendly Home, by David Pearson (Fireside/Simon & Schuster, 1996) This remarkable compendium has useful information for all country builders. It includes directories with sources of building materials, finishes, solar systems, water and waste systems, wood stoves, magazines and newsletters, and much more.

The New Cottage Home, by Jim Tolpin. (Taunton Press, 1998) You'll find 30 inspirational cottage designs. Many are simple backroad homes that enrich us, in Tolpin's words, "more with the highs of nature than with the highs of technology."

The Not So Big House: A Blueprint for the Way We Really Live, by Sarah Susanka and Kira Obolensky. (Taunton Press, 1998) Architect Susanka has a common sense concept: we should design and build homes with just the rooms that are used everyday. Her idea of a floor plan is one "inspired by our informal lifestyle instead of the way our grandparents lived."

Tiny Tiny Houses, by Lester Walker (Overlook Press, 1987) Forty small and simple homes presented in photos, plans and detail drawings by an architect who is an authority on American vernacular design.

Barns, Stables & Backyard Buildings

Building a Multi-Use Barn, by John D. Wagner. (Williamson Publishing, 1994) Builder John Wagner shows the versatility that's possible with one good barn. Using a 24' by 30' plan and simple framing, Wagner alters the interior layout to create a tractor garage and garden shed, a studio, a workshop and office, and a stable. His ideas should be considered by anyone looking for practical uses for old barns and heritage frames. Besides being a design guide, this book covers all the basics of light frame construction with easy-to-read text, photos and great illustrations.

Building Small Barns, Sheds & Shelters, by Monte Burch. (Story Books, 1983) From permits to the finish coat of paint, this book will guide you through your building process. Burch describes the advantages of different framing methods, roof styles and materials and backs his text with useful reference tables and concise construction details. The book presents plans for five small barns, two two-stall stables, a root and storm cellar, a carport, a tool shed, a woodshed, a smokehouse and shelters for hens, pigs and rabbits.

Complete Plans for Building Horse Barns Big and Small, by Nancy W. Ambrosiano and Mary F. Harcourt. (Breakthrough Publications, 1997) If you're planning to design or build a stable, you'll find yourself using this book again and again. It's a countrywide survey of creative designs for equestrian buildings. The buildings are presented with plans, photos and concise descriptions.

Horsekeeping on a Small Acreage: Facilities Design and Management, by Cherry Hill. (Storey Books, 1990) This common-sense guide, by a horse care expert, has information on planning your property, building design, fences, paddocks, fire safety, pasture and hay-lot management and much more. The book is packed with photos and with illustrations, plans and details of stable designs.

How to Build Small Barns & Outbuildings, by Monte Burch. (Storey Books, 1992) Burch combines great building advice with plans for 20 small buildings. You'll find designs for three small all-purpose barns, an eight-stall horse barn, various animal shelters, two garages and four garden sheds.

Low Cost Pole Construction, by Ralph Wolfe, with Doug Merrilees and Evelyn Loveday. (Storey Books, 1980) The classic guide is still a valuable introduction to the basics and history of pole building. It includes 290 photographs and illustrations and building plans for garages, small barns, a storage shed and a woodshed.

Practical Pole Building Construction, by Leigh Seddon. (Williamson Publishing, 1985) A complete builders' guide with reference tables, over 100 clear illustrations, photos and building plans for a lean-to animal shelter, a two-stall stable, a combination two-car garage and woodshed, and more.

Pole Building Projects, by Monte Burch. (Storey Books, 1993) This book presents the basics of pole building and design and includes plans you can build for barns, sheds, garden structures and garages. Useful tables, charts, photos and illustrations form a step by step guide.

Roofs and Rails: How to Plan and Build Your Ideal Horse Facility, by Gavin Ehringer. (Western Horseman, 1995) Ehringer covers all aspects of horse barn design and construction, from planning your acreage to hanging a halter. This book is filled with photos and easy-to-understand plans and details.

Rustic Retreats: A Build-It-Yourself Guild, by David & Jeanie Stiles. (Storey Books, 1998) Straightforward instructions and beautiful, informative drawings will help you build dozens of great back-country shelters. Designs include sheds, arbors, lean-tos, huts, cabins, tree houses and even a design for a floating cabin.

Sheds: The Do-it-Yourself Guide for Backyard Builders, by David Stiles. (Firefly Books, 1998) This book has the information you need to design and build your own ideal backyard shed. In fact, it serves as a great primer for any construction project. It covers planning, designing, permits, materials and construction methods. Stiles will guide you through the process, step-by-step, from the paper plan to hanging up your tools - in the shed you built! There are hundreds of great illustrations and projects you can try: a Victorian garden shed, cupolas, a Japanese boat shed, trash and recycling sheds, woodsheds, a pool pavilion and many more.

Fences & Walls

Building Fences of Wood, Stone, Metal, & Plants, by John Vivian. (Williamson Publishing, 1992) This is a general primer on building all types of fences and on growing hedges. The section on stone and masonry is particularly thorough. Great illustrations by Liz Buell, straightforward text and detailed photographs of works in progress make this a good resource for both novice and experienced builders.

Step-by-Step Outdoor Stonework, by Mike Lawrence. (Storey Books, 1998) Twenty different projects are presented in color photos and detailed drawings. Lawrence concentrates on patios, paving, steps, garden walls, stone furniture and decorative ponds. These are all projects that homeowners can handle themselves with this concise guide.

Stonework Techniques and Projects, by Charles McRaven. (Storey Books, 1997) A guide to the basics of stonework that concentrates on the most common projects: retaining walls, stone fences, foundations and steps, and then adds a bit more for the adventuresome: a fireplace, an arched bridge and a moon gate. A good book for the do-it-yourselfer or to learn what to look for in hiring a professional stone mason.

Yesterday's Country Designs

American Barns, by Stanley Schuler. (Schiffer Publishing, 1984) Take a tour of 240 old and new barns throughout the United States with this book's clear photographs and concise descriptions. You'll have a good introduction to our regional styles and to the amazing variety of different barn types. If you're planning to design or build a barn, you can't help but be inspired by the many photos of building details.

American Country Building Design: Rediscovered Plans for 19th Century Farmhouses, Cottages, Landscapes, Barns, Carriage Houses & Outbuildings, by Donald J. Berg, AIA. (Sterling Publishing, 1997) Some of yesterday's best designs are shown in original engravings, plans and in the words of their designers. Historic woodwork details and site planning techniques can help you design and build in the American country tradition.

Barns, Sheds & Outbuilding: Placement Design and Construction, Edited by Byron D. Halstead (Alan C. Hood & Company, 1994) This is a direct reprint of an 1881 classic, with a new forward by Castle Freeman. Halstead selected some of the most popular published designs from over two decades of the farm journal, *The American Agriculturist*. Designs include barns, stables, carriage houses, animal shelters, corn cribs, ice houses, spring houses, dog houses and bird houses.

The Farm: an American Living Portrait, by Joan and David Hagan. (Schiffer Publishing, 1990) Hundreds of color photographs document the American family farm and its passing way of life. Crisp shots and close-up details of beautiful barns, outbuildings and cupolas are sure to inspire your building project.

An 1881 farm cottage from the book,
American Country Building Design

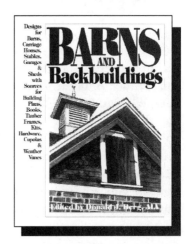

Index